SUNDAY SPARROWS

SUNDAY SPARROWS
星期天的麻雀

Selected Poetry of
Song Lin
宋琳

Translated from Chinese by
Jami Proctor Xu

Zephyr Press *&* The Chinese University of Hong Kong Press
Brookline, Mass | Hong Kong

Cover image by Xu Bing
Book design by *type*slowly
Printed in Hong Kong

This publication is supported by the Jintian Literary Foundation.
Zephyr Press also acknowledges with gratitude the financial support
of the Massachusetts Cultural Council.

massculturalcouncil.org

Zephyr Press, a non-profit arts and education 501(c)(3) organization,
publishes literary titles that foster a deeper understanding of cultures
and languages. Zephyr Press books are distributed to the trade in the U.S.
and Canada by Consortium Book Sales and Distribution [www.cbsd.com].

Published for the rest of the world by:
The Chinese University of Hong Kong Press
The Chinese University of Hong Kong
Sha Tin, N.T., Hong Kong

Cataloguing-in publication data is available from the Library of Congress.

ZEPHYR PRESS
www.zephyrpress.org

JINTIAN
www.jintian.net

THE CHINESE UNIVERSITY OF HONG KONG PRESS
cup.cuhk.edu.hk

CONTENTS

Translator's Foreword

I met Song Lin at the very first poetry festival I attended in China in 2008. The festival was held in Tongli, an ancient town with waterways and arched stone bridges not far from Suzhou. I ended up sitting at Song Lin's table at the opening night banquet. The now deceased poet Zhang Zao was there from Germany, and he and Song Lin were talking about their experiences living in Europe. They invited me to go to Lake Tai with them the next evening, but I somehow missed going with them. When they returned, Song Lin's face was bright with excitement as he told us about walking along the shore at night and describing the moonlight on the water. "You have to go there sometime," he said, telling me of the lake's size and about the Lake Tai stone's use in traditional Chinese gardens. The next day as the poets walked around Tongli, Song Lin said we needed to walk with the poet Gao Xing, because Gao Xing grew up nearby and he could tell us stories about the bridges and buildings. Later that night, we were two of the poets who went to a local karaoke bar at one a.m. to sing, dance, eat fruit, and continue the conversations that had been flowing all day. Song Lin got out his sketchbook and showed me some drawings he'd done. Later he sang "Moscow Nights" in Chinese. When I moved to Beijing later that year, Song Lin and I became close friends almost immediately, and we spent a lot of time together at poetry and art events in Beijing and around China. Those days in Tongli were my first introduction to Song Lin as a poet, artist, and a person.

Song Lin is a combination of poet, artist, wanderer, storyteller, and philosopher. All these aspects are woven through his poetry as well as his daily life. In some ways, he seems to exist outside of time, but it's because he's inhabiting several times at once. He once told me, "Sometimes I feel like someone from antiquity. So many ancients live inside my body, and looking at the world and creation through their eyes, I see so much disappearing, but I haven't disappeared. I still exist." Standing beside a pavilion in Yangzhou, he's just as likely to be reminded of a story about an emperor and his concubines from the Sui Dynasty as he is to be lost in conversation with the gardener tending to the flowers. And both of these might later end up in the same poem. Song Lin has traveled much of his life, and he's absorbed the histories, landscapes, cultures, and literatures of the various places he's lived.

His life has also been a mixture of idyllic moments, transitions, and deep traumas. He was born in 1959 in Xiamen, Fujian, but was raised by his maternal grandparents in Qibu Village, in Fujian Dongshan District. He says that the rural landscape and folk customs there shaped his childhood worldview, and that his grandfather's kindness and his grandmother's Buddhist beliefs helped to nurture gentleness in him. When he was ten he went to live with his parents in Ningde, Fujian. He wrote his first poem in middle school and became infatuated with poetry after his father encouraged him in his writing. His mother died from an illness when he was fifteen and his father was imprisoned the following year due to a factional struggle during the Cultural Revolution. In 1977, his father was sentenced to death under the baseless charge of "Destroying the Knowledge of Youths Sent to the Countryside." During this time, Song Lin had graduated from high school and had been sent to the countryside as an educated youth himself; he was treated unfairly due to his father's situation. He was forbidden from taking the college entrance exams two years in a row, but when he was finally allowed to take them, he was accepted into East China Normal University's Chinese Department in Shanghai.

During college, he helped establish the Summer Rain poetry club and began publishing his poetry in 1981. After graduating, he stayed on as faculty and taught writing. Song Lin has said that when he moved to Shanghai, he experienced the shock Benjamin describes people experiencing when they first encounter big cities, and he wanted to write about the city in his poetry. He was inspired and guided by Shi Zhecun, who was his teacher and later his colleague. Shi was one of the earliest and most prominent urban writers in Shanghai in the 1930s, and he edited the modern literature journal, *Les Contemporains* (现代). In addition to Shi, Song Lin also began reading poets such as Baudelaire, Elliot, Rilke, and Borjes in translation. In 1987, his first poetry collection was published in *Urbanites*, a collection of poems by four poets that is seen as a representative work of 1980s Chinese urban poetry. In 1989 Song Lin participated in the democracy protests in Shanghai and was sentenced to nine months in prison. He wrote poems in prison to grapple with the uncertainty of not knowing when he would get out. The title poem of this collection, "Sunday Sparrows," is one such poem. After his release, he was stripped of his teaching qualifications and became a librarian in the Chinese Department. He immigrated to France in 1991 and later studied ancient Chinese philosophy at the 7th University in Paris. He left Paris in 1997 and lived in Singapore and Argentina before returning to China in 2003 to teach at various universities.

I began this project several years ago when Song Lin and I were both living in Beijing and he asked me if I would be willing to translate a collection of his poems. I jumped at the chance, and we spent many days during the next several months meeting to go over his poems.

When I translate the work of contemporary poets, I translate a rough draft of the poem and then meet with the poet to talk about the poem before revising my translations. With some poets, this process is fairly quick, but Song Lin and I would often spend several hours together and only get through one poem, or we would get to telling stories and forget to do any poems. Other times we spent several hours on one poem while Song Lin told me the background story of the poem, the emotional/mental state he was in when he wrote it, and/or the literary and historical allusions in the poem. Or we would spend an hour discussing the meaning of a particular word. Two of Song Lin's nicknames are Song Zhenman (Song is Really Slow) and Lao Manye (Old Slow Grandpa). This is due to his tendency to show up several hours late for dinners or parties—again, this is related to how he exists within and beyond "modern time." Once I was at a birthday party he'd invited me to and he showed up four hours after it started. After he arrived he began telling stories and later played his bamboo flute. Song Lin is beloved even for his perpetual tardiness. I have a tendency to lose track of time when I'm involved in conversations, or to lose track of projects while I'm busy traveling for events. This combination meant that this project happened off and on for several years and spanned different cities once Song Lin moved to Dali to paint and write full time and I moved to the US and was traveling back and forth across the Pacific. But this project has been a labor of love for me the entire time, not only because it deepened my friendship with Song Lin, but because his poems are weavings of history, myth, nature, city, everyday life, melancholy, joy, story, image, and classical and modern Chinese.

—*Jami Proctor Xu*

Acknowledgments

Thank you to the editors of *Left Curve*, *Ambush Review*, and the Chinese University Press, who published some of these poems.

Thank you to Song Lin, for his friendship and for all the conversations we shared during the translations and revisions. Thank you also to my dear friends Zhang Yuehong and Caroline Knapp, who read the earliest versions of the translations; Lucas Klein, who meticulously read a portion of the poems; Christopher Mattison, who edited the manuscript with detail and care; and Lydia Liu, who first introduced me to the world of contemporary Chinese poetry when I was her student at Berkeley, and who read through the manuscript last summer. My translations benefitted from the invaluable suggestions made by each reader. Thank you to Jack Hirschman, Charis Thompson, Kari Boyd McBride, Yoon Sook Cha, Jonathan Stalling, Denis Mair, Melissa Mack, and many others for support, guidance, and advice. Thank you also to friends and family who encouraged me at various stages of the project, especially to Dylan, Zoe, Simon, and my parents.

SUNDAY SPARROWS

星期天的麻雀

只有时间

只有时间是真实的
只有时间能穿越表象世界的感官进入体内
让坐在藤椅中的女人仅仅转动一下脸庞
　　　便使观赏者的眼睛惊异
　　　使你彻夜不眠

只有时间创造了流动
　　　创造了河
两只水獭被自然之母丰腴的子宫分娩
爬上岸来频频交颈
宇宙由此进化
这无知的兽类是颅骨硕大的人的先哲
　　　也是最初的观察者

只有时间使香樟树凿成不系之舟放浪于泽上
　　　午宴的男人和女人隔着巨川
　　　看见我们
　　　相继远去
留下了承接果实的火制陶盘
由聪慧之手举过头顶
只有时间具有如此巨大的挑逗性
　　　向你亮出最神秘的部位
　　　又迅疾遮掩
只有时间的喉腔发出尖锐而怪诞的声音经久不衰
　　　在你的血流里激起水花
　　　万物在舞蹈中静止

Only Time

Only time is real.
Only time can enter the sense organs of the world of representation
and enter the body
It makes the woman in the rattan chair turn her face slightly
      and astonish the one who sees her.
      It makes your whole night sleepless.

Only time creates flows
      and rivers.
Two otters are born from Mother Nature's womb.
They crawl onto the banks and embrace.
This is how the universe evolves.
These ignorant animals were the precursors of large-skulled people.
      They were also the earliest observers.

Only time hews the camphor tree into an untethered boat
that floats on the pond, unrestrained.
      The river separates us from the men and women
      at the lunch banquet. They watch us
      recede into the distance.
The earthenware plates of leftover fruit
are lifted over our heads by clever hands.
Only time is this immensely tantalizing.
      It flashes its mysterious parts at you
      then quickly conceals them.
Only time's throat lets out a freakishly shrill sound
      that splashes in your blood flows
      and renders all living things immobile mid-dance.

只有时间让那么多远道而来的朝觐者双膝着地
普利高津的前额被欲望敲出黑洞

在世界的海滨
不明飞行物的残骸长成一片
                                    人间奇景

只有时间端坐于高坡
用灿烂的手指向我耳语
人啊，举在我右手上的地球是一只多味苹果
内中的果仁有三颗
时间如是说

Only time makes all people kneel down after distant
journeys for an audience with the emperor.
Desire knocks a black hole in Prigogine's forehead.

UFO wreckage
on the shores of the world
            becomes a marvel in the human world.

Only time sits erect on high slopes
and uses its magnificent fingers to whisper to me:
Man, the world I hold in my right hand is a succulent apple.
It has three seeds inside.
This is what time says.

流水

跪下的人，从望远镜背后看见天象
一只蝎子倏忽而过，咬住一把石釜，空气在颤动
他手中吉祥的蝴蝶也飞入烟尘
如流水
行止何处呵，蝎子，做客的好人
栈房里堆放着木头，深山的鳞光涂在车轮上
有如张开的嘴
为你的远游点燃火把

给一匹快马洗浴的裸身闯入大海
被谁所摄像？额前挂满了水
城市中动作迟缓的庸人在博物馆的门洞里
等待最后一分钟营救
那马群已死，火车的履带滑向深谷
是大地在动吗？
太阳在天外啸叫。是天空在动吗？
谁说：要有人，于是就有了人
谁在无声无息中煤气中毒

被遗弃的荒岛周围流水涣涣，吸入我们有罪的身体
我们不知道一切，正如高贵的水漏不知道我们
裹尸布上有一束暗红的花
散落如金
但我们终于记住了，不可能回来的去处，可能回去的来处
梦中打着手势的呓语，道破玄机
集体自杀的鲸鱼吐出最后一片沙滩
永恒的征兆高挂云帆

Flowing Water

The kneeling man observes celestial phenomena through the telescope.
A scorpion rushes past, bites into the stone cauldron, and the air trembles.
The auspicious butterfly in his hands flies into smoke and dust,
like flowing water.
Where should he end his journey, this scorpion, the good-hearted guest?
There's wood stacked in the inn. The pearlescence deep in the mountain
      is smeared
onto tires, like an open mouth,
that lit a flame for your distant journey.

Who films the nude bathing the horse rushing into the sea,
his forehead covered in water?
The sluggish commoners in the museum doorway
wait for a last-minute rescue.
That pack of horses has already died, the train wheels have already slipped
      into the ravine.
Was this because the earth moved?
The sun whistles forlornly outside. Is the sky in mourning?
Who said: Let there be people, and then there were people?
Who was quietly poisoned by gas?

The flowing water around the island evaporates, and our guilty bodies
      breathe it in
We don't know anything, just like the water clock doesn't.
We have a dark red flower on our shroud;
its petals scatter like gold
but we've finally remembered the places from and to which we can't return.
Gesture-filled sleep-talking in dreams, profound theories revealed,
whales who've committed mass suicide spitting out the last section of beach,
the eternal omen on the high-flying cloud-sail.

但我终于收到了唯一的那封信
邮戳像屁股上的胎记，轻轻托在妈妈的手心
蝎子呵，妒嫉的飞虫
离开你不可占卜的轨道到这里来
我踏上亿万光年的滑梯，从层层脱去的躯壳里
从煤层下的岩洞之门的一道裂缝
妈妈诞生过我的手心也颠覆着我
记住她生前所有的灾难
万象如流水。我们
在眼睛和耳朵之间睡去，因有限而不可企及

But the only letter I end up receiving was placed in my mother's hand.
The postmark is like a birthmark on the buttocks.
Scorpion, you jealous insect,
leave the trajectory you can't divine and come here.
I step onto a slide millions of light years long
from all the layers the body has shed,
from a crack in the stone cliff below the bed of coal.
My mother gave birth to me with her hands and flipped me over.
I remember all the disasters from when she was alive.
Every phenomenon is like flowing water. We
fall into sleep between our eyes and ears, we
can't be striven for because we're unsurpassable.

空白

在那里时间解放了我们。一只翅膀最红，
遮着世界，而另一只已轻柔地在远处扇动。
——埃利蒂斯《勇士的睡眠》

去过的地方离我们并不遥远
憋足了气慢跑就能赶上。一些容颜古旧的鸟
胸脯里装满谷粒
我的口袋里装满了钱
去白得耀眼的房顶上滑雪
跌落时会有一阵恐惧的心跳，脚发软
身体的下面很深
晚上在铁道旁的旅店里光着身睡眠
隔着栅木可以看见
肌肤若冰雪
方寸之间有一丛绒毛粘上福分
与窗外灵性的草没有两样
无声地漫延
直到月蚀，天上出现空白

那一切都挨得很近
火柴和烟斗，腰和臀，宗教和艺术
两个半圆轻轻合起
像下巴上的嘴，用呼吸吹奏死亡
最美的花在城市附近的村舍微笑
没有人知道她的身世
父王的脑髓被神明点了天灯
我想起枫丹白露之夕
画匠们拖着雪橇云集，争论什么是空白

Emptiness

There time released us. One wing, the reddest,
covered the world, while the other gently fluttered in the distance.
—Odysseus Elytis, "The Sleep of the Brave"

The places we've been aren't far from us.
Holding my breath and jogging I can catch up. Some archaic looking birds
have their chests stuffed with grains.
My pockets are stuffed with money.
I go to the dazzling white roof to ski.
As I descend my heart pounds with terror and my feet go weak;
the snow is far below.
At night we sleep naked in the inn beside the railroad tracks.
Separated by a fence, we can see
flesh like snow.
Between hearts there's a clump of fur with happiness stuck to it,
which is no different than the spiritual grass outside the window,
spreading silently
until the eclipse comes and an emptiness appears in the sky.

All that was close together:
matches and pipes, waists and buttocks, religion and art
two semi-circles gently coming together
like the mouth on the chin, using breath to play death.
The most beautiful blossom is smiling in a cottage near the city.
No one knows her life history.
The sky lantern in the king's brain is lit by the gods.
I think of a Fountainbleau evening—
the craftsmen in the painting are crowded together, pulling sleds, debating
        the meaning of emptiness.

房客有了主人——这是我的财产
你们随便使用吧
午夜的另一面是墙壁，突破
你可以继续赶路
我把手枕在头下，身体便缓缓飘过
所有去过的地方
城市的停尸房里有我的熟人
绰约若处子
可怜的脚涂满了泥巴，手松开一片死光

The tenant has a landlord—this is my property.
Use it as you please.
The other side of midnight is a wall—break through it
and you can keep hurrying along.
I rest my hand on my head, and my body slowly drifts past
all the places I've been.
The morgue has people in it I know,
graceful maidens,
pitiful feet smeared with mud.
Hands let loose a tract of death.

一船被贩运的少女之歌

那条船已驶出港湾。
下午，我乘长途车抵达这座城市。
刺桐树，叶子碰着叶子，
塔，对称着苍翠的远山。
我站在石桥上，海水低平。
偷渡者的船就是这样
冒着黑烟并开足了马力。

无数巧合中的一种。风景
浑圆地在我的视网膜上展开，
波浪被螺旋桨撕成条状。
我在人群中，被空气推搡着，
像一个视入太阳的盲人。

为此我痛恨过自己。
在旅馆客房里，
你慷慨的柔情接受了我有罪的躯体。
皱巴巴的报纸一角，我又见到了它，
满帆，超重，不可一世，
几乎越过我的头顶。

那一夜我们手牵手逛遍每条街，
沉浸在死亡的亢奋中，
那么快地把自己的姐妹遗忘在了海上。
她们将同压舱物呆在一起，
始终比想象超出半海里。
故乡之岸在最后一瞥中
倾斜，同一个月亮
升上了台湾海峡。

A Song for the Girls Smuggled on a Boat

The boat sails out of the harbor.
I arrive in this city by bus in the afternoon.
On the coral trees, leaves collide with leaves.
The pagoda stands symmetrical with distant green hills.
I stand on the stone bridge, the seawater flat.
The smuggler's ship runs
at full horsepower, emitting black smoke.

This is one coincidence among many. The scene
unfolds in full across my retinas,
propellers shred waves into strips.
I stand among the crowd, pushed and shoved by the air
like a blind man gazing at the sun.

I've hated myself for this—
In the hotel room
your generous tenderness accepted my guilty body.
In the corner of the wrinkled newspaper, I saw the boat again,
at full sail, overloaded, arrogant.
It seemed to sail over my head.

That night we held hands and walked through the streets,
soaked in the excitement of death.
How quickly we forgot our sisters left at sea.
They were pressed against the ballast
half a nautical mile further at sea than we'd imagined.
In their final glance, their hometown shore
was slanted; the same moon
rose above the Taiwan Straits.

星期天的麻雀

我真想唱一支麻雀之歌
飞越一步之遥——那小小身体的火
一个冒险的念头
是多么敏捷地钻进了云层

一阵风之后，天空现出无数亮点
仿佛一片骤然的阳光压迫
树——它摇晃着，又迅速
克制住疯狂的晕眩

我真想留住这一个时刻
跟一只麻雀的对视
长如隔世的等待。让镜子的幻觉
持续到真实的梦境来临！

鸟类中的凡夫俗子
短短的羽毛覆盖住笨拙的决心
当灾难的预感迫近，空气里
传来阵阵雷鸣

像是主施瞌睡的天使
借宿于檐下，对着一隅长天发呆
哦！麻雀，真想再为你唱一支歌
但我早已是饥肠辘辘

Sunday Sparrows

I really want to sing a sparrow's song
That small body's flame flies across the distance of a footstep
A risky idea
so agilely burrows itself into the clouds

After a gust of wind, innumerable points of light appear in the sky
as if abrupt sunlight is oppressing the tree
The tree sways then rapidly
regains control over the wild vertigo

I really want to hold on to this moment
when the sparrow and I gaze at each other for the length
of time it takes to wait a lifetime. Let the allusions in the mirror
persist until the real dreamland arrives!

Commoners among birds
with short feathers covering a clumsy determination
When premonitions of disaster draw near, claps
of thunder come ringing through the air

It's as if all the angels in charge of sleep
have asked for lodging beneath the eaves and they're staring blankly
into a corner of long sky. O, sparrows, I want to sing a song for you
but I've been aching with hunger for so long

海上的菊

把镜中发芽的种子撒在海上
把剑收起来。剑
在海水里冒着热气
菊花烂漫，满架的书倾倒
一面镜子同时飞出三只夜莺
是什么东西惊魂未定
谁在一只漏气的橡皮艇上惊魂未定
我的喉咙接住空中落下的一柄剑
我横空出世，复又下沉
梦游于海上的仙山和明月

Chrysanthemums on the Sea

Sprinkle the seeds sprouted in the mirror onto the sea
Put the sword away. The sword
is emanating heat in the seawater
The chrysanthemums are in bloom; the books have fallen off the shelves
Three nightingales simultaneously fly out from the mirror
What is this that feels so frightened and shaken
Who is it on the leaking rubber boat, so frightened and shaken
My throat catches a sword falling from the sky
From the firmament, I enter the world, then sink back down,
sleepwalking among mountains of immortals and the bright moon above the sea

选自《死亡与赞美》

2

听不见她心中喧嚷的蜂房
阳光下忧郁的少女。我只是用手听
在通往春天的走廊尽头
她站立，像一面睡在风中的旗

绛色蜜蜂的旗使空气里
充满火药。而外面，清新的蔷薇园
从她肩膀的轮廓消失了
蔷薇的骨朵似乎布置了更紧张的气氛

蜂房，啊嗡嗡鸣叫的阳光
幽闭了少女，烦恼使她如同大地的牛乳
流淌在青春秘密隐藏的地方

这明快和侧面的美穿来穿去
与死亡订立了契约的少女
心中的蜂房代替她把忧郁倾诉

5

我们对死亡的道理所知不多
正如对事物本身的困难所知甚少
当手握住鸟的影子，手飞翔
而尺度又把手握在它的手里

from Death and Praise

2

I can't hear the buzzing hive in her heart—
the melancholy young woman in sunlight—I can only use my hands to listen.
At the end of the corridor that leads to spring
she stands like a flag asleep in the wind.

A crimson flag fills the sky
with gunpowder. And outside, the pure rose garden
disappears from the outlines of her shoulders.
Rose buds seem to adorn an even tenser atmosphere.

The hive and the buzzing sunlight confine
the young woman. Distress makes her become like earth's milk
flowing into the hidden places of youth.

This sprightly profile of beauty passes back and forth.
The hive in the heart of the girl who signed a contract
with death pours out melancholy for her.

5

We know very little about the principles of death
just as we know almost nothing about the difficulties of objects.
When a hand grabs hold of bird shadows, it flies
but then measurement grabs that hand in its hand.

深深陷入失败，恸哭
一盏鹤腿上的灯带领石头飞翔
突入遗忘的领域，是什么高明的尺度
使我们回到倾听的兴趣？

河中的石头梦见岸上的石头
鸟远离立在水面的月亮
银灰之夜的美人用美貌驱散了黑暗

蛇与百兽翩翩起舞
大乐师，一边行走，一边吹箫
尺度在白昼的空谷落下金色的羽毛

21

啊！五月使我们
忘记春天。明媚的光芒中
第一个人倒下了。他的宽肩膀
那蓝色希望号军舰的甲板

倾斜，在歌声中完全沉没了
带着他内心信仰的饥饿
和脑子里最后的幻念。空气散开
仿佛被深深划了一道刀口

他的身体在继续倒下
另一些，他的另一些身体被光芒碾碎
六月的车轮高大，黑黢

"不要拿走我爱人的生殖器！
不要拿走我的爱情！"当那女人
祈求，我们全都流下了眼泪

Sinking into deep defeat and crying in grief.
A lantern on the crane's leg guides stones in flight
and quickly enters the forgotten realm. What brilliant measurement
will lead us back to our interest in listening?

The stones in the river dream of the stones on the riverbank.
The birds are far from the moon that stands on the water's surface.
The beautiful woman of the silver-gray night uses her beauty to disperse darkness.

All creatures begin a graceful dance with snakes.
The great musician plays the flute as he walks
and measurement sheds gold feathers in daytime's empty valley.

21
May makes us
forget spring. The first person collapses
in brilliant rays of light. His broad shoulders
are the deck of the warship Blue Hope.

He tilts sideways and sink into the song's sound,
carrying his heart's hunger for belief
and his mind's final illusions. The air separates
as if a blade has cut deeply across.

His body continues its collapse.
The others—his other bodies—are pulverized by light rays.
June's tires loom, pitch black.

"Don't castrate my lover!"
"Don't take away my lover!" As she
pleaded, we all wept.

感恩

灰尘在大地上跳跃
树、汽车和头颅在大地上跳跃
一首挽歌在大地上跳跃

没有更高的事物
群山之上一览无余
只剩下一座浩渺的建筑，里面
居住着心，破碎后重整的心
在大地上跳跃
酒在大地上跳跃，船只绕过死海
回到故乡的港口
人们站在山顶也感到如此渺小
捧出鲜花般的心相互比较

大地上亿万座房屋在跳跃
厚厚地覆盖着地球

Gratitude

Dust hops on the ground.
Trees, cars, and heads hop on the ground.
A dirge hops on the ground.

There is no higher object.
As far as the eye can see,
all that remains on the back of the mountain is one splendid
building. Hearts are living inside it. Broken and mended hearts
hop across the ground.
Alcohol hops on the ground. Boats only pass by dead seas
on their way to their home ports.
People feel so paltry standing on mountaintops.
They hold out their hearts like flowers and compare them.

Billons of houses hop on the ground
thickly covering the planet.

野蛮人自画像

不过我刚刚踏上你的领土——
劳伦斯·斯特恩

我站在圣竿下面
因此我看不见大天使

一个波兰人在手锯上奏出音乐
塞纳河流逝掉秘密的好时光

风格一分一秒地牺牲
铜马、铁桥、骑在激情之上的

蓬乱头发。内心一滴血
把我向虚无的星空放逐

哦，掌声在古剧场回荡
哦，不丹的神灵带上了面具

我来自一片黑夜的废墟
我要为一切悲恸的心灵祈祷

这个长着一只角的怪物
在欧洲的视线里还未生养下来

Self-Portrait of a Barbarian

But I have scarce set foot in your dominion—
—Laurence Sterne

Because I'm standing below the sacred rod
I can't see the great angel.

A Polish man plays a song on a saw.
The Seine River carries away secret good times.

Style is sacrificed every second.
A copper horse, a metal bridge, matted hair riding

on passion. A single drop of blood in the heart
banishes me to the night sky of emptiness.

Applause rings out in the theater.
Bhutanese gods don their masks.

I come from the ruins of a dark night.
I want to pray for all souls in mourning.

This one-horned monster
hasn't yet been born in Europe's line of sight.

缅怀

在火山口
一群喀斯特形状的人被烧成灰
这些满怀基督教忧郁的早年圣徒
要在幻想的领域建立一座
最后的殉道者村庄
夕阳西下，羊群如同书页翻动
那留在废墟上的几个窟窿
像一所永不开学的信仰的学校

Commemoration

At the mouth of the volcano
a group of karst-shaped people were burned to ashes.
These early saints replete with Christian melancholy
wanted to build a final martyrs village
in the domain of delusion.
The sun sets. Livestock are flipped like pages of a book.
The few remaining caves on the ruins
are like a school of belief that won't ever open.

蒙巴那斯的模特儿

一件看不见的东西有多重？
比如眼球上一个细孔的疲倦

海突然想穿过一条鱼
看一看那边是什么水域

在被画出来以前
鱼变成孔雀石以前

黑暗沉睡于比子宫更窄的空间
造物者的手掌也难在里面飞翔

模子自己醒来，向大地俯冲
有如成熟的梨从梨茎上脱落

就在这里持续着，凭吊着眼泪
但没有隐衷，也没有哀怨

从睫毛开始的大火如此骇人
连一粒雀斑也不剩下

她会不会找回满头乌发？
像箜篌在郊外墓穴里鸣响

冰山会不会停止移动？感官
会不会在宁静的夜晚从墙上飞走？

一株昔日樱桃树等在花园里
当蜜蜂吮吸肖像上她金色的阴影

Montparnasse Model

How heavy is an unseen object?
For example, a pore of fatigue on the eye

The sea suddenly wants to pass through a fish
to see what waters lie on the other side

Before the sea is painted,
before the fish turns to malachite

Darkness is fast asleep in a space narrower than a womb
It's hard for the creator's hand to fly inside

The mold awakens on its own and dives toward the earth
just as a ripe pear falls from the stem

Merely persisting here, paying homage to tears
but without hidden sentiments or plaintiveness

The fire that begins from her eyelashes is so destructive
not even a single freckle remains

Will she recover her full head of crow-black hair
like the *konghou* peeling in graves on the outskirts of town?

Will icebergs stop moving? Will the bodily organs
fly from the walls on a quiet night?

A cherry tree from the past waits in the garden
while the honeybee sucks her gold shadow on the portrait

弱音区

动物梦境的郊区无人管辖
只有天空一个邻居。雪压屋顶。

电线杆，麻雀线上的生活，
以五十音步的节奏弹拨二月。

一切来得正是时候，
好天气在坏天气里休止。

一封寄自故乡的信三次把我叫醒，
黑沙在途中继续把它书写。

被罚的奴隶请进门烤一烤手，
天空没有你也会有别人支撑。

Pianissimo Area

There aren't any human administrators in the suburbs of animal dreams;
the sky is the only neighbor. Snow weighs down the roof.

Electric poles and sparrows' lives on the wire
pluck February's strings using a fifty-foot cadence.

Everything comes at the right time.
Good weather ceases in bad weather.

A letter from my hometown wakes me three times.
Black sand continues writing it along the path.

Slaves who've been punished, please come in and warm your hands.
If you don't hold up the sky, others will.

母亲唱给保育箱中的婴儿

小小的玻璃房，不系之舟，
你降世者的避难所，
在夜的刀光剑影下漂流。
你的呼吸那么微弱，
你轻如一枝风信子。

躺在隔离怀抱的地方，
吮吸不到母亲的乳房，
你的手悲哀地握紧。
千万不要松开手，儿子！
不要害怕闪电的长蛇。

如果黑夜女巫掠走你，
不要让她的汤勺
碰你干渴的嘴唇；
午夜，到了她魔法的地带，
更别让她对着你吹气。

到处是暗礁和水草的陷阱，
你该多么小心呀，
该懂得哭声会召来不幸。
况且一点点恶意的波浪，
就能把你的身躯覆盖。

这是你诞生的世界，
你别无选择的世界。
你需有耐心，当风暴过去，
星星的火将来温暖着你，
梦将告诉你你是谁。

Mother's Song for Her Child in the Incubator

Little glass house, untethered boat,
your refuge for those born floating
beneath night's knife light and sword shadow.
Your breath is weak,
you're weightless as a hyacinth.

You lie in a place separated from embrace,
unable to suck on mother's breast.
Your hands sorrowfully hold on tight.
Don't let go, son!
Don't be afraid of lightning's long serpent.

If the witch of the dark night sweeps you away
don't let her ladle
brush against your parched lips.
At midnight, when you arrive in her magic field,
don't let her blow on you.

Reed and waterweed traps are everywhere.
You have to be careful, you must
understand that cries summon misfortune,
and that even small waves of evil intention
can cover your entire body.

This is the world into which you were born,
the world you had to choose.
You have to be patient. When the storm has passed,
the fires of stars will warm you
and dreams will tell you who you are.

儿子，要用天赋去识别
沿岸的各种标记。
活过这一夜就是胜利！
漂过来吧，到黎明这边来，
看，曙光女神抱起你。

Son, you must use your gifts
to discern the signs along the shore.
To live through this night is a victory!
Float this way; come toward dawn.
Look, the goddess of dawn light is holding you.

正午的邂逅

在呛人的阳光里停下脚步
突然，一个飞人落在山毛榉树上
悠然自得的平衡术被大海的磁场搅乱
——我是他冒险记录的偶然见证

鸟屿，这些在时光中浣洗的
白昼的星辰，正午的漫游者
犹如闪光的额头沉思着一步棋
沙兰特河用多棱镜照着它们

或许他就是那棵想飞的山毛榉树的
一个梦，通过枝叶的摇篮回到大地
如果他曾经绽开也是在天空中
毕竟那降落伞是用幻象织成

看他身轻如燕地走向海滨大道
仿佛已从教训中脱胎换骨
那里一个少女正仰脸把他迎接
她的花园像荨麻阴影里的罗盘

"请问这个村庄叫什么名字？"
"永恒的恶魔之夜"
"这么说我误入了水妖的王国？"
"是的，我们等你来已等白了头"

隔着篱墙你一言我一语
海上的风暴在邂逅者头顶悄然聚集

Noon Encounter

My steps cease in the suffocating sunlight.
A flying man suddenly lands in a beech tree.
A natural balancing technique is thrown off by the ocean's magnetic field—
and I'm a witness to his risk-taking feat.

Bird Island: these daylight stars wash themselves
in time; noon sleepwalkers
seem to have flashing foreheads pondering a chess move.
How many prisms does the Charente River use to reflect them?

Perhaps he was the dream of the beech tree who wanted to fly,
to return to the earth in a cradle of branches and leaves.
If he bloomed before, this also took place in the sky.
After all, that parachute was woven with illusions.

I see him walk toward Oceanside Boulevard, light as a swallow,
as if he's already been reborn from past lessons learned.
A young woman looks up and greets him.
Her garden is like a compass among the nettle shadows.

"Excuse me, what's the name of this village?"
"Night of Eternal Demons."
"You mean I've accidentally entered the realm of sirens?"
"Yes. We've waited for you for so long our hair has gone gray."

Separated by a hedge, he says one thing and she replies.
The storm over the sea gathers silently over the head of this man
        I've encountered.

水壶

从水壶中的黑暗到躯体的黑暗，
是浑然不觉间来临的夜。
我划亮火柴，坐回桌前，
回忆起日落前写下的诗中的一行。

夜更深了，山上有雪，
崖边那颗星被擦洗得更加明亮。
从黄昏起它就在那儿漫游，
它大概渴了，像一只蟋蟀沉寂下来。

现在只有水壶在独自歌唱，
像厨房里的蟋蟀呼唤另一只
荒野的蟋蟀。它也在呼唤我的嘴唇，
去轻触温暖的、雪水茶的芳菲。

多奇妙，一只水壶，从不问我是谁，
随时都能给我安慰。
哟优美的弧形，妇人般的柔顺，
水倾出又倾入，欠缺了又满盈。

而我知道，有一个匠人打制了这只
不知年代、灰色曲柄的水壶。
我熟悉孤寂中的欲望之渴，
倘若我出门，它或将伴我远行。

Kettle

The darkness in the kettle, the darkness in my body
are a night that comes without warning.
I light a match, sit down at the table,
and remember a line from a poem I wrote before sunset.

Night deepens; there's snow on the mountains.
The star beside the precipice is scrubbed even brighter.
It's been wandering since dusk.
It's probably thirsty, like a cricket growing silent.

Now the kettle sings alone,
like a cricket in the kitchen calling
to a cricket in the wild. It's also calling for my lips
to gently touch the scent of warm tea brewed with melted snow.

It's wondrous—a kettle that never asks who I am
can always bring me comfort
with its graceful arches and feminine suppleness. The water is
poured out and poured back in; the kettle is emptied then filled again.

And I know that a craftsman forged this
gray-handled kettle from some other era.
I'm accustomed to the thirst of desire in loneliness.
If I leave home, perhaps it will accompany me on the long journey.

飞蛾的行动

灯下独坐，面对纸的空白，
就像一个失去记忆的人面对钢琴，
不知如何弹奏，苦恼于尚未出现的曲调，
又沉醉于那个曲调，整夜
被朦胧的预感所控制。
外面，某种声音敲打窗子，
要求进来。一只，两只，三只
　　　　　　　飞蛾撞击着，猛烈而急迫，
像风暴中雪花的运动，
像进入大气层后流星的最后行旅。
火的不速之客，自毁的一族，
做着死亡练习——意念之死亡。
但飞蛾与灯焰之间的玻璃似乎更为强大，
冷漠，透明，幽光闪烁，
像意志中的残忍看守着虚无
　　　　　　　和距离的冰川。
一阵风打开了窗子——
　　　　　　　猝不及防，飞蛾把自己加入灯焰，
　　　　　　　用全部的力量加入灯焰，
　　　　　　突然，准确，一次就实现。灯光
放大的瞬间，影子在墙上颤抖不已。

Moth Movements

I sit alone beneath the lantern, facing the blank page
like someone who's lost his memory facing a piano,
not knowing how to play, distressed by the melody that hasn't yet come,
but also intoxicated by that melody. I'm
controlled all night by a vague sense of foreboding.
Outside a sound raps at the window
and asks to enter. One, two, three
                moths strike fiercely, urgently—
the action of snowflakes in a storm,
the last journey after a meteor enters the atmosphere.
They're fire's uninvited guests, a species of self-destroyers
practicing death—the death of ideas.
But the glass between the moths and the lantern seems to become
more powerful, indifferent, transparent, a faint light flashing
like the cruelty of will that guards the glaciers
            of nothingness and distance.
A gust of wind opens the window
      Before it can be prevented, the moths join the lantern's flame.
      They use all their strength to join the flame
      suddenly, precisely, succeeding in one try. The instant the flame
increases, the shadows on the walls shudder and tremble.

扛着儿子登山

我们的皮肤是群山和空气的朋友，
我们的嗅觉是一只羚羊的朋友——
在一棵小橡树上它留下气味。

我们坐下休息，村庄看不见了，
隐居者的房子静悄悄的。
雪线那边，裂缝中有一副死鸟的细骨架。

方型烟囱，蓝色的窗子，
一小片菜地是甲壳虫和蜜蜂的家园，
人在粗糙的土墙上留下掌模。

我们走向湖区，群山也一样，
随着太阳的升高群山变得更高了，
光圈像一只只轮子，在叶子上滚动。

超级的水晶倾泻而下。浓云的色彩
搅入轰鸣的瀑布的色彩。
我们向着洞穴发出野兽的吼叫。

Climbing a Mountain with My Son on My Shoulders

Our skin is the friend of mountains and air.
Our sense of smell is an antelope's friend—
it leaves its scent behind a small oak tree.

When we sit down to rest the hamlets are beyond our view
and the hermit's houses are silent.
There along the snowline, a slender bird skeleton lies in a crevice.

Square chimneys, windows with blue frames,
a vegetable plot that's home to beetles and honeybees,
people have left handprints on the coarse earthen wall.

We walk toward the lake and the mountains
also follow the rising mountains, becoming taller in the sun.
Circles of light are wheels rolling on leaves.

The super crystal pours down, and the colors of thick clouds
are stirred into the colors of the bellowing waterfall.
Facing the cave, we roar like animals.

城墙与落日

——给朱朱

在自己的土地上漫游是多么不同，
不必为了知识而考古。你和我
走在城墙下。东郊，一间凉亭，
几只鸟，分享了这个重逢的下午。

轩廊外的塔，怀抱箜篌的女人，
秦淮河的泊船隐入六朝的浮华。
从九十九间半房的一个窗口，
太阳的火焰苍白地驶过。

微雨，行人，我注视泥泞的街，
自行车流上空有燕子宛转的口技，
雾的红马轻踏屋顶的蓝瓦，
我沉吟用紫金命名了一座山的人。

湖，倒影波动的形态难以描述，
诗歌一样赤裸，接近于零。
对面的事物互为镜子，交谈的饮者，
伸手触摸的是滚烫的山河。

我用全部的感官呼吸二月，
我品尝南京就像品尝一枚橘子。
回来，风吹衣裳，在日暮的城墙下，
快步走向一树新雨的梅花。

The City Wall and the Setting Sun

—For Zhu Zhu

It's so different to walk on one's native land;
you don't need to verify the past. You and I
walk below the city wall. The eastern suburbs, a pavilion,
and a few birds share in this afternoon of our reunion.

A woman holds a *konghou* in the wooden corridor
and the Qinghuai River boats are hidden in Six Dynasties ornamentation.
The sun's flame faintly gallops past
one window among ninety-nine and a half.

Soft rain. Pedestrians. I gaze at muddy streets while swallows'
vocal mimicries wind in the air above the flow of bicycles.
Fog's vermillion horses tread lightly on blue roof-tiles.
I wonder who named the mountain Purple-Gold.

It's hard to describe the way the reflections ripple on the lake.
Poetry is equally bare, approaching zero.
The objects across from us become our mirror: people drinking, talking.
They hold out their hands and touch the scalding landscape.

I use all my organs to breathe February in;
I taste Nanjing as if tasting a tangerine.
I've returned; the wind blows my clothes. Below the city wall at sunset
we walk back toward a tree-full of plum blossoms in spring rain.

告诉云彩

一个个尖顶刺入天穹，一排排浪翻滚，
轮辐和磁针都不会停止，欲望也不会。
我们活在世间，抛开苦难不谈，
走在街上，大步流星，依然先前模样。
梅花看过了蟋蟀歌声又起，
月光浣洗金棕榈的绸衣，和我们
神圣夏夜的欢爱，燕子倾斜，
有点娇慵的人儿多妩媚。
诗人下地狱，与亡魂交朋友，
而市侩们抹着嘴唇，站成一圈，
拥着蜂腰或蛇腰进出转门。

现在你看，西天那一抹彤红的云彩，
幻美，灿烂，点燃了银行大厦的玻璃，
也把绿光的圆弧镶入松鼠的眼睛。
我为何不能赞美这哀伤的天使，
这回光之海的惊心动魄，
这可见的移动的乐园，奇迹人生
短暂的万花筒？我为何要去想，
我有多孤独，多厌烦，多绝望，
像那些入夜以前将客死他乡的人，
像哈姆雷特？就这样告诉漫溢的云彩，
说我们已来到阳台，且啜饮又观望。

Tell the Clouds

Spire after spire point into the firmament, row after row of waves roll.
Wheel spokes and magnetic needles won't stop, neither will desire.
We live in this world, not speaking of suffering,
and we walk with large strides, the same as before.
Once we see plum blossoms the crickets' song begins again.
Moonlight washes the palm trees' silk clothing and our mystical
summer night love. Swallows slant.
The languorous dear is so lovely.
Poets descend into hell and befriend dead souls
while philistines wipe their mouths, stand in a circle, and come and go
through the revolving door, their arms around slender waists.

Look at the red clouds in the western sky.
Their brilliance sets the windows of the high-rise bank ablaze
and embeds arcs of green light in squirrels' eyes.
Why shouldn't I praise this grief-stricken angel?
This breathtaking reflected light?
This visible shifting paradise? The ephemeral kaleidoscope
of this miraculous life? Why should I think
of how lonely, frustrated, and hopeless I am,
like all those who die in foreign lands,
or like Hamlet? Just tell the overflowing clouds
we've already come to the balcony, taken sips, and looked out.

透过鹰眼看见的风景

1

只有岩石和雪
黑色和白色。
隆冬，河不再流动，
松树套上玻璃罩子。

2

岩石的高度，
山峰的高度，
不可能被任何东西所替代，
除非被大雪所覆盖。

3

一群群雨燕沉睡在冰河下面，
洞穴里，棕熊沉睡，
土拨鼠和刺猬也深深睡去，
体内堆满脂肪的雪。

4

没有词语，没有兜售词语的人，
没有婚礼或权力的赞歌。
在西藏，一支军队陷入雪中，
被月亮的遗忘所埋葬。

Landscape Seen Through an Eagle's Eye

1

There are only rocks and snow,
black and white
Deep in winter, the river no longer flows
Pine trees don glass nets

2

The rocks' height,
the peaks' height
can't be replaced by anything
except what snow covers

3

Flocks of swifts sleep beneath the frozen river
In caves brown bears sleep soundly
and groundhogs and hedgehogs fall into deep sleep,
their bodies piled full of fat like snow

4

No words, no peddlers of words,
no paeans to marriage or power
In Tibet, an army sinks in snow
gets buried by the moon's forgetting

5

风是灵感，意志
是飞行中血流的速度。
阴影移动，然后
爪子猛然抓破寂静

6

必要的简化，像残枝和败叶
被土地所简化，像岩石，
孤独地耸立，灿烂地耸立，
成为一切感觉的基础。

7

即使在冻结的雪野上，
也遍布太阳黑色的导火索。
透过鹰眼看见的风景——
一首有关距离的诗。

5

The wind is inspiration; determination
is the speed at which blood flows in flight
The shadow moves, then
claws suddenly break the quiet

6

Necessary simplification, like fractured branches and withered leaves
simplified by the earth, the way rocks
tower alone, tower in splendor
and become the foundation of all feeling

7

Even the frozen plain of snow
is completely covered by the sun's black fuse
A landscape seen through an eagle's eye—
A poem about distance

外滩之吻

1

外白渡桥上，你发梢的风
阳光细碎，你看着来来往往的船只
黑披肩裹得更紧了。我熟悉
模糊的，一闪而过的脸
汽笛，据说纯属于感伤的发明
短促的，像冬天的咳嗽。我们
说着话，很慢，先是你，然后是我
我想起大学时代，从黄昏开始
恋人们就倚着江堤接吻
穿过树的密语，瑟瑟响，瑟瑟响
而在城南那些特殊的夜晚
一个人因为失去名字
发现自己原本是另一个人
他躺着，躺在那远去的、烟囱喷出的
声音上面，冻得倦成一团

2

记得吗？从花店出来我吻了你
我们终于没去找那条街
而是又回到外滩，这样很好
重新开始那未完成的，刚才我说什么啦？
光的印象。是的，钥匙的光
水缸内壁上那种摇荡的光
闭起眼睛感觉到被缓缓推向前

Kisses on the Bund

1

On the Garden Bridge, the wind in the ends of your hair.
Sunlight fractures. You watch the boats come and go,
your black shawl wrapped more tightly around you. My familiar
face passes in an instant, indistinct.
It's said the steam whistle was purely a melancholic invention,
fleeting, like a winter cough. We
speak slowly—first you, then I.
I think of college, when beginning at dusk
lovers leaned on the causeway and kissed.
Secrets rustled and rattled past trees.
During those anomalous nights in the southern part of the city
a man discovers he is someone else
once he loses his name.
He lies there, lying on the sounds
from the steam whistles that disappear into the distance.
He's curled up, frozen.

2

Do you remember? I kissed you when we left the flower shop.
We ended up not looking for that street
and returned to the Bund instead. That's good,
starting over what wasn't finished. What did I just say?
Impressions of light. Yes, the light of keys,
the rocking light on the inner walls of the water jug.
I close my eyes and feel myself slowly being pushed forward.

愿谅我用过那个腥膻的比喻
苍蝇，吊死鬼的天花板
门突然大开，灿烂使人
睁不开眼睛，太阳，涡伏的
我想把它够着，它摇晃着
咣的一声，被沉重的板隔开了
躯体像木刻，颓然倒下
手只好贴着墙，就这样用手听着外面。

3

这张照片上的人像我
蹲坐着，随处可见的，劳者的姿势
车身翘起，车柄触着地面
Hurry, hurry, 他已耳熟能详
背、毛巾、小腿的弹簧，还有心跳
我们听不见的，经常被略过了
令人难堪的本土特色，对不？
惟有他的目光是捕捉不住的
天气很好，在敞蓬的黄包车前
他看向这边，筷子和碗
比能说出的更多。时间魔术
还会从杯旧的帽子里拉出什么？
吊袜带、短而宽的袖子、白手套
喷香的纸扇，从桥上跑下来
在拐角稳住车。优雅的
二郎腿小姐欠起身，递过一个施舍
挥挥手，打发了一段行程
总感觉那种目光没有死
围拢而来，麻木的，像沉默的深井

Forgive me for having used a rank metaphor.
Flies, and the ceiling where dead ghosts hang.
When the door suddenly opens, it's too bright
to open my eyes. The sun is a spiral.
I want to grab hold of it, but it's swaying.
There's a slam, then we're separated by a heavy board.
My body topples over like a wood statue.
All I can do is put my hands on the wall;
I use them to listen to the world outside.

3

The person in this photograph looks like me.
He's squatting in the pose so typical of workers.
The rickshaw carriage is raised up, the handle is touching the ground.
"Hurry, hurry," he recites in the English he's heard so often
                    he's memorized it.
His back, his towel, the springs in his calves and
his racing heart we can't hear—Aren't these
the often overlooked unbearable aspects of our homeland?
Only his gaze can't be captured.
The weather is nice; he looks this way
from in front of the rickshaw. His bowl and chopsticks say more
than words could. Will time's magic
still be pulled out of the old hat?
Suspenders, short wide sleeves, white gloves,
and a scented paper fan. He comes running down the bridge,
steadying the rickshaw as it turns the corner.
The elegant woman with her legs crossed lifts her body; she hands
over alms, waving her hand to send off that stretch of her journey.
It seems that this sort of gaze still hasn't died:
people crowding around, numb, like a silent deep well.

4

我们沿着江边走。人群，灰色的
人群，江上的雾是红色的
飘来铁锈的气味，两艘巨轮
擦身而过时我们叫出来
不易觉察的断裂总是从水下开始
那个三角洲因一艘沉船而出现
发生了多少事！ 多少秘密的回流
动作、刀光剑影，都埋在沙下了
或许还有歌女的笑吧
如今游人进进出出
那片草地仿佛从天外飞来
你摇着我，似乎要摇出盼望的结论
但没有结论，你看，勒石可以替换
水上的夕照却来自同一个海
生活，闪亮的、可信赖的煤
移动着，越过雾中的汹涌
我们依旧得靠它过冬

5

街灯亮了，看不见的水鸟
在更高的地方叫着，游船缓缓
驶离码头。你没有来，我犹豫着
终于还是坐在观光客中间
喷泉似的光柱射向夜空
钟楼的庞大阴影投在回家的行人身上
"夜上海，夜上海"，芸芸众生的海
奇异的异乡漂流的感觉，一支
断肠的歌。不管在何处
我仅是一浪人而已

4

We're walking along the river. Crowds of people, gray
crowds of people. The fog over the river is red,
and the scent of rust floats over. We yell as two large ships
brush past each other. Ruptures not easily perceived always begin underwater.
How many things have happened on this delta because a sinking ship arrived?
How many backwards currents, movements, flashing knives
and sword shadows lie beneath the sands,
and perhaps even the laughter of singsong girls.
Now tourists come and go.
This stretch of grass seems to have flown from outer space.
You're shaking me as if you want to shake out a hopeful conclusion,
but there is no conclusion. Look, stone monuments can be replaced
but the glow of the sunset on the water comes from the same sea.
Daily life and sparkling, reliable coal
are moving, passing through waves in fog.
We still rely on it to get through winter.

5

The streetlamps are lit and the waterfowl we can't see
chirp from even higher places. Tour boats slowly
sail away from the dock. You haven't come. I'm hesitating,
but still end up sitting among the tourists.
Beams of light shoot like fountains into the night sky.
The bell tower casts its giant shadow over the people walking home.
"Shanghai nights, Shanghai nights." This sea of living beings,
a strange feeling of drifting in a foreign land, a heart-
breaking song. No matter where I am,
I'm just a vagabond.

恍惚之城，但愿现在能够说
我回来了。往昔的恋情隐入
星光的枝叶，我需要更多的黑暗
好让双眼适应变化。当对岸
新城的万家灯火沸扬，我靠着
船尾的栏杆，只想俯身向你

Trancelike city, I wish I could say
I've returned. Past love is hidden
in the starlight's foliage. I need more darkness
so my eyes can adjust to the changes. As the thousands
of lights in the houses on the opposite bank sizzle, I lean
against the rail at the back of the boat. I just want to lean towards you.

致可能的外星人

亿万年之间，群星诞生，群星死去。
仰望星空的人在夜晚看见的
不过是感官的镜像，
内心的诸多渴望之一。

夜凉如水，要有一扇窗，让未眠人
斜倚着沉浸在天体的气氛中。
思念赋予她，心灵的无穷奥妙，
赋予他勇气，静息等待。

要有一座桥，横越银河的汹涌，
要有一夜，照亮别的漫漫长夜。
亿万年之间，或许你终会听见
织女的杼机或牧牛郎的一声哀叹。

天上人间，最最遥远的距离
也许是两个人——从你到我。
星星与我们究竟是什么关系？苍白的火
燃起我们身上陌生的恋情。

透过太平洋上空红色的云雾，
今夜我在一条船上阅读星图。
星光的崎岖路，灿烂而甜蜜，
你快来吧，乘上飞碟向我飞来。

To a Likely Alien

For millions of years, stars were born and stars died,
but those who gazed into the night sky merely saw
a mirror image of their sense organs,
one among a multitude of their inner desires.

The night is cool as water. A window is needed to allow
the reclining insomniac to soak in the celestial body's atmosphere.
Her longing endows her spirit with limitless subtleties
and gives him the courage to wait quietly.

A bridge is needed to traverse the violent surges of the Milky Way.
A night is needed to illuminate other endless nights.
Over the course of a million years, you might finally hear
the weaver girl's loom shuttle or the ox-herder's sigh.

The greatest distance between heaven and earth
might be that between people—from you to me.
How are the stars really related to us? A pale flame
ignites an unfamiliar love.

Tonight I'm on a boat reading maps of the stars
through the red clouds over the Pacific sky.
The rugged road of starlight is resplendent and sweet.
Hurry, come to me on a flying saucer.

选自《多棱镜，巴黎》

1

绿叶中有喷泉的眼泪循环
五月的街头画家，我欣赏他把明亮部分
处理成天使。它太高了所以你不能
叫它趴下；无性，因而徒具光辉
早晨的太阳是初生的婴孩
如果你赞叹那云的浓艳
雾的色情，就不必在天体中寻找
未来的祥瑞，过去的奇迹
你曾经滔滔不绝，如今为何黯哑？
水边的乡愁吹皱了月亮
风之谜响彻我记忆王国的幅员
陌生的事物犹如彩绘玻璃
镶嵌的技艺，半明半昧
这想象的神秘形态超越逻辑
和夸夸奇谈。如果你听见枝头
嫩芽的呼唤，你就是春天
但天使仅属于命名的一种
羽翼拍动，地狱应声粉碎

3

观看或冥想，带着原始欲望
和所有人一样活在浑浊的世上
在乌托邦和死亡的阴影中
风车倾斜着。上方是塔，再上方：群星
但下面，皮卡尔的老鸨在拉客

from Multi-Prism, Paris

1

The fountain's tears circle among green leaves.
I'm admiring the way May's street artist has painted the bright section
into an angel. Because it's too tall, you can't
tell it to bend over; because it's genderless, all it has is radiance.
The morning sun is a newborn baby.
If you praise that cloud's vibrant colors
or the fog's eroticism, you don't need to search
for future omens or past miracles in celestial bodies.
You used to talk incessantly; why have you fallen silent now?
The homesickness at the water's edge blows ripples in the moon.
The wind's enigma resonates through my memory of the kingdom's territory.
Unfamiliar objects are like stained glass:
the art of embedding both the translucent and the opaque.
These imagined mystical forms transcend logic and exaggerate fantastic tales.
If you can hear the shouts of buds on branches, then you are spring.
Angels belong only to one kind of naming.
When wings flutter, hell's reply shatters.

3

Watching and meditating with original desire
in this turbid world of shadows
between utopia and death.
The windmill slants.
Above it, there's a pagoda, and above that, there are stars.
But below, Pigalle's madame is soliciting customers.

你需要学会保持一段距离
看人们怎样行事，拒绝或逢场作戏
像那个用报纸裹一枝花的伪绅士
洗衣妇船，艺术家的圣地
这些台阶似乎通向一个秘密天体
孤独丈量我，厌倦的虚无
她舞蹈而来，踢踏尖叫
刀刃般裸露，像一只光芒四射的孔雀
她用最激烈的方式布道：
"胜任快乐，然后给予快乐"
这弗洛依德的女信徒
像我一样，是短暂的、必死的
却无意间揭示了一条真理

You need to learn to keep some distance,
to watch how people act: either refusing or joining in
like the fake gentleman who wrapped a flower in newspaper.
Le Bateau-Lavoir, the holy land of artists.
These stairs seem to lead to a secret celestial body.
I'm measured by solitude and the nihility of boredom.
She comes dancing over, tapping and shrieking,
naked as a knife-blade, a peacock sparkling in every direction.
She preaches in the fiercest manner:
"You'll be given happiness once you're qualified to be happy."
This Freudian convert
is as fleeting and mortal as I am,
but she's inadvertently revealed a truth.

江阴小调

1

躺在亭子里的人
睡着了
他的两个朋友变成两条鲟鱼
第三个变成蝴蝶，飞入芦花
他梦见云朵
像盛世的仪仗行列
倒映在水面上
他梦见徐霞客
远游归来

2

阳光中的橘树玲珑如玉
不缺乏思想，并不缺乏天堂的感觉
隐逸的芒刺忍受着霜、雪
叶脉呼应叠起的江潮，习习微风
满足于此时此地，满足于
在光的神经中晕眩

3

江船顺流而下时
江水仿佛漫上了月亮
正是清明时节
儿童在岸上奔跑
灯笼颤颤悠悠
像死者的眼睛朦朦胧胧

Jiangyin Ditty

1

The man in the pavilion
falls asleep.
Two of his friends are transformed into sturgeons.
The third is transformed into a butterfly, and flies into the reed catkins.
He dreams the clouds
are a procession in a golden age
reflected on the water's surface.
He dreams Xu Xiake
has returned from his distant journey.

2

The orange trees are like jade in the sunlight.
They don't lack ideas, and they don't lack heavenly feelings.
Secluded barbs endure the frost and snow.
Leaf veins mirror river currents. The breeze
is satisfied in the here and now; it's satisfied
to become dizzy in light's nerves.

3

As the boat goes downriver
the water seems to flood the moon.
It's grave-sweeping time.
Children run along the river bank
and the trembling, swaying lanterns
are like the eyes of the dead

照着溺水的歌妓
或王朝的传说
向下漂流

4

没有闪闪发光的绫袍
没有门帘上的小银钩
可以透过香喷喷的松枝窥视
一个诗人毁了
接着，又一个诗人
须髯从云端投下
蓝色或红色的影子

5

无非是怪石的诙谐
为庭园增添了情趣
无非是修篁、翠柳
给他们以温柔
你和我勾留，寻找
难免风尘仆仆
沉醉于肉体押韵的诗

dimly shining on drowned singsong girls
or on the legends of dynasties
floating downward.

4

There aren't any shiny silk gowns,
and there aren't any silver hooks on door curtains
to be seen peeking through fragrant pine branches.
Once one poet is destroyed
another poet's beard casts red or blue shadows
from high in the clouds

5

It's simply a matter of artificial stone hills
increasing the courtyard's appeal.
It's just the tall bamboo and green willows
providing them with tenderness.
You and I pause, searching.
We're rushed as dust in the wind,
intoxicated by poems of rhymed flesh

在拉普拉塔河渡船上对
另一次旅行的回忆

这水域几乎不能称之为河，它宽得像忘河
一同渡河的人却不一定同归
赫拉克利特感叹过，孔子感叹过
但不容争辩的河流说着它自己的箴言
因为河流乃是大地的舌头
太阳照见船舱里几个爬来爬去的婴儿
城市在一瞥中像一个模糊光斑的恐龙
船尾的人感觉要站得稳些
河流被用来命名逝者，人就只能在岸上
目送、踏歌、深情缅邈地祝福
我想起长江，曾经是界河的另一条河
在镇江和古瓜州之间，在意识的同样
开阔的水域，你和我谈着话
沉思着，试探着将要抵达的对岸
我们的嘴唇贴在了一起

Thinking of Another Journey While
on a Rio de la Plata Ferry

This body of water is so wide it almost can't be called a river; it's so wide
       it's as wide as the Lethe,
but someone who crosses a river with you doesn't necessarily return with you.
Heraclitus lamented this, Confucius lamented this,
but incontestable rivers speak their own maxims
because rivers are the earth's tongues.
The sun shines on several babies crawling around the cabin.
At a glance, the city looks like a dinosaur with glowing spots.
The people at the back of the ferry feel as if they should stand more steadily.
A river is used to name the dead, and all people can do is stand along the banks,
bidding farewell with their eyes, singing and stomping their feet,
with deeply-felt blessings sent afar.
I think of the Yangtze, and how it also used to be a river on the border
between Zhenjiang and ancient Guazhou, a body of water
as vast as this. We're speaking to each other,
reflecting, feeling out the bank at which we'll arrive.
Our lips are pressed together.

给青年诗人的忠告

也许这就是诗：飞矢之影
反对飞矢的运动。遵循着
天方夜谭的逻辑，大象从容
穿过针眼；对于逝者，濠梁之鱼
有它高出一筹的理解
它们倏尔游动，或止息静观

大师难觅，知音即使在世上
某个地方，此刻常缺席
例如，困惑的伯牙来到渤海岸边
竟然为无情的泡沫而销魂
于是，他弹奏的已不是原来的古琴
谁是那绝响？我们只需聆听

哲学对你如无助益，最好
直接去寻访秋天的山石
水落下去，石，坚定而充实
君子般坦荡。沿着溪涧缓缓攀登
刘晨与阮肇，就是这样在山中
邂逅了如花似玉的仙女

Advice for a Young Poet

Perhaps this is poetry: a flying arrow's shadow
fighting against the movements of the flying arrow. Following
the logic of the Arabian Nights, an elephant easily passes through
      the eye of a needle.
Fish in the Haoliang River possess a superior understanding.
They swiftly swim, or they pause and observe.

Great masters are hard to find. Even if the one who truly hears your music is
somewhere on this earth, in this moment they're often absent.
For example, when the bewildered Bo Ya arrived at the shore of the Bohai Sea,
he was unexpectedly enraptured with the merciless foam.
Therefore, the *guqin* he played was no longer his original one.
Whose was that final music? We just need to listen.

If philosophy is of no help to you, you should
go directly to look for autumn's mountain rocks.
Water flows down but rocks are resolute and substantial;
they're magnanimous as gentlemen. Climb slowly
along the stream, this is how Liu Chen and Ruan Zhao
encountered an immortal woman as beautiful as jade.

脉水歌

——重读《水经注》

1

大河在远方闪烁，犹如一道
来自北极的光。太阳的火舌下
羿的箭矢穿过云的旗幡
我移动，像《山海经》中的测量员
雁阵在蓝天书写一个人字
流水浣洗着林壑的耳朵
在我的衣襟前制造一个节日
飞瀑在悬崖绝壁激起回响
一条又一条河穿过我的躯体
帝国的通都和彩邑中有我的驿站
美人因迟暮而忧伤，醒来
衣袖空留昨夜的余温

2

岸草青葱尾随我远去
而生活本是在岸上筑居
为什么要告别笙歌和画舫
去追逐蛮荒的河流？
为什么骑驴，饮风，偃蹇而进
易水而弱水，塞北又江南？
漫长的行旅中，孤独已变成
心的刺客。夜半客船上
家书的炉炭烘暖我的双手
出发的日子，话别的时刻而今安在？
凶年又加上不驯服的河道
星星的沙粒壅塞平原

Song of Exploring the Waterways

—Rereading *Commentary on the Water Classic*

1

The great river glistens in the distance like an aurora.
Yi's arrows pass cloud banners
under the sun's flamed tongue.
I move like a surveyor in the *Classic of Mountains and Seas*.
A formation of geese writes the ideogram for person in the blue sky
Flowing water washes the ears of the forest ravine
and creates a holiday on the front of my silk robes.
The flying waterfall echoes over the sheer cliffs.
River after river passes my body.
There are hitching posts for me in imperial Tongdu and Caiyi.
The beauty mourns her faded youth, and when she awakens,
all that's left is last night's warmth in her sleeves.

2

Riverbank grasses and greenery follow me into the distance
yet life builds its home on the riverbank.
Why do we leave behind flute songs and pleasure boats
to chase the savage river?
Why ride a donkey, drink the wind, grow weary and enter
the Yi or Ruo Rivers, Saibei or Jiangnan?
On a long journey, loneliness becomes
the heart's assassin. At midnight on the passenger ship
the charcoal of letters from home warms my hands.
The day of departure, the moment of farewell, and where am I now?
Famine years and untamed rivers,
star sands congest the plains.

3

死亡的黑车满载兵器
烽火中的白马连翩西驰
曙光像秘件的封泥那样火红
大河从贫瘠的远方流来
经过同战争一样贫瘠的土地
那么多人在饥饿中死去，又在死后梦见
玉蜀黍和干葡萄，梦见女人们云集
辩认着比冻土更僵硬的自己
手在空中掘墓：苍天！苍天！
她们像怀中婴儿般号叫
那么多等待化为乌有
好似干戈化为玉帛

4

倘若青鸟来过，曾栖于什么枝头？
罗盘搜寻到哪一座仙岛或灵山？
裸国残缺，怪物的想像同样残缺
龙族的血液里有它们的低语、尖叫
《禹贡》山水犹在，贡船早倾覆
接着走来了游侠，纵横家
和篡位者仪仗中大象雄武的步伐
这片土地的传说，河流的传说
像炭黑的赤壁被烧得滚烫
像石上的勒文，只有风能够识读
连同智者的浩叹都将化为乌有
影子交错，有谁曾抵达过彼岸？

3

Death's black chariot is loaded with weapons.
White horses in beacon-fires gallop west in succession.
Dawn is the same blazing red as the seal on secret documents.
The great river flows from the barren distance
passing an earth as barren as war.
So many have died in that hunger, and after they died,
dreamed of grapes and corn, dreamed of women gathering
to see themselves stiffer than the frozen earth.
Their hands dig graves in the sky: *Heaven! Heaven!*
They cry out like infants being held.
So many wait to become nothingness
like weapons of war becoming jade and silk.

4

If the black messenger bird came, on which branch did it alight?
Which Immortal Island or Soul Mountain did the compass find?
When Naked Country is battered, monsters' imaginations are also battered.
The dragon people's blood holds their whispers and screams.
The mountains and rivers in *Yu Gong* still remain, but the boats
        with imperial offerings sank long ago.
Then come the knights-errant, the strategists,
and the bold elephant-like march of the usurpers.
The myths of this land, the myths of this river
like the coal black Red Cliffs being burned
like engravings in stone only the wind can read.
Together with the deep sighs of sages, they will all become nothingness.
Shadows intertwine, yet who has been to the other shore?

5

渔父调舟而去，桂棹轻点
抛下一支恼人的《沧浪歌》
多事之秋的高树用伤疤的瞎眼眺望
我走过的泥足深陷的路
一只蝴蝶被尘土压住有无原由？
一只萤火虫为我照明是否出于自愿？
除了继续早已开始的仰观俯察
泾属渭汭的清浊，南北分流的盘根错节
现在岂不是一一稽考的时候？
说，即便最终等于不说
像流星的湮灭，石棺的沉默
铁函有朝一日会浮出深井

6

云梦泽上的云，销魂的雨
宋玉的解梦术满足了楚王的淫欲
清水之畔，筼篁幽幽，名士们
伴醉、打铁、冶游于林中
与残暴的君主旷日周旋
我又怎能幸免侍者的头衔
在奉命陪同皇帝北巡的游历中
梦想山川风物和美的人心
从一部水之书发现了不得已之境
我岂不愿放浪于市廛之间
像绿鹦鹉，在烛光的妩媚中
在玄奥中谈吐世道陵迟

5

The fisherman turns his boat around and departs, gently dipping
        the cassia oars
casting off an annoying Song of Cang Lang River.
A tall tree in a troubled autumn surveys the scene with eyes of scars,
the road I walked where my feet sunk deep in the mud.
Was a butterfly crushed for no reason?
Does the firefly shine for me of its own will?
In addition to surveying the clear and muddy bend
where the Jing and Wei Rivers converge,
the complications of which flow north or south,
how is now not the time to inspect them all one by one?
To speak, in the end, is the same as not speaking,
like a meteor's annihilation, the silence of the sarcophagus.
One day the metal letters will float up from the well.

6

The clouds above Yunmeng Lake, ecstatic rain.
Song Yu's dream interpretation skills satisfied the King of Chu.
Clear water's edge, serene bamboo, literati gentlemen
feign drunkenness, forge iron, and go courting in the woods,
wasting time mingling with the cruel king.
How did I narrowly escape the title of attendant,
ordered to accompany the emperor north,
dreaming of scenic mountains and streams and beautiful hearts?
I discover the boundary of coercion in a book of water.
How could I be unwilling to loiter in the market,
metaphysically talking about the decline of the times
like a green parrot in the charming candlelight?

7

开创的人物，天之骄子
遥远如来自某个河外星系
沿着倾斜的日影下凡
敷土，祭奠高山，命名了百川
那传说中的水王不曾回来
广漠掩埋迟到者的悲哀
河与人喧响两种孤寂
一如那不可能停下的箭矢
惟有脉跳还在呼应地下的涌动
惟有记忆汇合成更辽阔的河
当我踌躇着不知该向何处去
月亮那水的魂魄引导我

8

经典已朴散。在扭曲的时代
我只想做一个脉水人
在精心绘制的地图上规划
一度是桃花源，后来是战场的山水
渴时我就以朝圣者的姿势弯下腰
风像色情的山鬼挑逗我：
看啊，一切皆流。但重泉中
我的影子却如如不动
变化多端的四季的仪表
涨落的水文，让我徒然兴叹
并连连发问：什么样的钩沉索隐
可以追回遁走的暗流？

7

The first human, the pride of heaven,
distant, as if from another galaxy,
descended to this earth along the slanted sun shadow,
laying out soil, offering sacrifices on the mountain,
              and naming the hundred rivers.
That mythic king of the waters has never returned.
Vastness buries the sorrow of those who came late.
Rivers and people resound with two kinds of loneliness
like the unstoppable arrow
only arteries echo underground surges,
only memories converge into wider rivers.
When I hesitate and don't know where to go,
the moon, that water spirit, guides me.

8

The Classics have been altered. In a twisted age
I just want to be an explorer,
to plan on a meticulous map.
Once there was the Peach Blossom Spring, then a battlefield terrain.
Thirsty, I'll bend forward in a pilgrim's posture
and the wind will titillate me like an erotic mountain ghost.
Look, everything is flowing, but in the layers of the spring water,
my reflection seems motionless.
The appearance of the ever-changing seasons,
the fluctuating hydrology makes me gasp in vain with joy.
I ask again and again: What sort of lost references
can bring back the fleeting undercurrents?

9

这是一则轶事，这是流亡
漫长的行脚从一个龙忌的字开始
只带上很少的必需品
走着，一个人不仅可以梦见
爵禄、荣名、弄臣的粉墨
可以洗手不干，可以懒卧
也可以远走高飞。没有禹迹
只有银色的丝涎那徐缓蜗牛的
逶迤哲学。对我而言，远
就是近；走，就是用交替的脚踵
量尽河流的长度，大地的幅员
停步倚杖，在峻湍边看云

10

急迫的鹰唳叫着，唳叫着，唳叫着
大地之鹰，展翅在云端
那声音像黄昏天空的一个亮点
神秘的河图的一个疑点
像从殷墟飞来的传奇的巫祝
戴着面具，发出预言：
"旅者，你该向视域外搜寻
在倾听中配制魔咒的力量
你也该知道源头的涓滴原本弱小
逆流而上即与那一脉活水为邻
梦想的颠踬也是生活的颠踬
当大河上的彩虹横绝远空"

9

This is an anecdote, this is exile.
A long trek beginning with a word a dragon deems taboo.
Only bringing a few necessities.
Walking, not only can one dream
of nobility, glory, and becoming a favored imperial servant,
he can also wash his hands of this and lie down,
or he can fly far away. There are no traces of Yu;
there's only the silver thread giving birth to that slow snail's
winding philosophy. For me, distance
is closeness, walking is alternating the heels
to measure the length of the river and the area of land.
Pausing my steps, leaning on my staff, I look at the clouds from the torrents.

10

The urgent eagle is calling, calling, calling.
The eagle of the earth spreads its wings in the clouds.
The sound is a bright spot in the dusk sky,
a dubious spot on the mysterious river chart
like the legendary shaman who flew from the Ruins of Yin
wearing a mask, offering a prophecy:
"Travelers, you should search beyond vision
and create the power of magic in listening.
You should know the stream that comes from the source is weak at first,
but if you walk upstream, you'll get close to the flowing water.
Stumbles in dreams are stumbles in life
when the rainbow over the river cuts across the distant sky."

布洛涅林中

湖水的碎银，在巴黎的左侧
狮子座越过火圈。

松针，你的仪式道具。

风数你变灰的头发，
睫毛，影子凌乱的狂草。

桨，沉默之臂划过蓝天，
兜着圈子，干燥像孩童挖掘的沙井
在梦之岸坍塌下来。
呼吸与风交替着，
串串水珠的松林夕照
挂上隐居者的阁楼。

巨人头颅，无人授受，
磨亮渡口的老钟远在西岱岛，
敲打死囚的回忆。

火鹤，你渴慕的竖琴，
弹拨湖心。
彩虹里盲目的金子挥霍着，
覆盆子的受难日，
林妖现身于马戏团，
爻辞之梅酸涩，
没有归期。

In the Bois de Boulogne

Broken silver on the lake; on Paris' Left Bank,
Leo passes through a ring of fire.

Pine needles, your ceremonial props.

The wind counts your graying hairs,
your eyelashes, wild grasses with shadows in disarray.

Oars, those silent arms, paddle across the blue sky
moving in rings, dry as the wells children dig in sand
that collapse into the banks of dreams.
Breath alternates with wind.
The pine forest sunset hangs strings of dewdrops
from hermits' attics.

No one accepts the giant skull.
The old clock at the polished ferry crossing is far away on the Ile de la Cîté,
ticking against death row memories.

The flamingo is the harp for which you thirst;
it plucks at the lake's heart.
The blind gold in the rainbow is squandering
the Good Friday of raspberries;
the forest monsters appear in the circus;
the trigram's plums are sour;
you have no return date.

从水圈到水圈，
星的王冠被夜叉击碎。

铁塔下边走来一个亡命者。

The crown of stars is smashed by Yaksha,
from hydrosphere to hydrosphere.

A fugitive walks over beneath the iron tower.

南疆札记

1. 莽荒的上帝读着沙漠的盲文。
2. 库车之夜，我收到火星拍来的电报：这里曾有水的痕迹。
3. 死去的河流像扭曲的干尸，在天空的陈列馆里。
4. 语言，尘埃中的尘埃，在漫漫长路上飞扬。
5. 桨，立在船形棺前。沙海的水手，告诉我，你梦想着什么样的航行呢？
6. 商旅的驼队向东，向西，太阳烘烤着眉毛、胡子和馕。
7. 走。一旦躺下，你将冒着被风干的危险。
8. 从看不见的边界到边界，我细数那些消失了的国度。
9. 有一只蚕梦见过罗马，或相反，罗马梦见过一只蚕。
10. 胡杨林里的微风：丝与瓷的谐音。
11. 汉公主刘细君——乌孙国的萨福，嫁给了广袤无边的乡愁。
12. 在鸠摩罗什的塑像下，我想到，也许是他晓畅的译文拯救了佛教。
13. 前往长安朝觐的三大士，走着与三博士相反的路径。
14. 设若汉武帝知道，汗血马是一种病马，《大宛列传》是否将改写？
15. 壁画上的供养人有着细细的眉眼。
16. 佛塔——沙漠导航系统。
17. 多么大的遗憾！甘英看见了海，却不知是哪个海。
18. 曼佗罗花瓣——一枚枚五铢钱。

Notes from Southern Xinjiang

1. The god of the jungle is reading the desert's Braille.
2. One Kuchar Nahyisi night, I receive a telegram from Mars: This place once had traces of water.
3. The dead river looks like a contorted mummy in the sky's exhibit hall.
4. Language is dust within dust flying upward on the endless road.
5. The oar stands upright in front of the boat-shaped coffin. Tell me, sailor in the desert sea, what kind of sailing do you dream of?
6. Merchant camel caravans head east and west. The sun roasts their eyebrows, beards, and *naang* flatbreads.
7. Keep walking. As soon as you lie down, you're in danger of being dried out by the wind.
8. Between the invisible border and the border, I'm counting the countries that have disappeared.
9. A silkworm dreamed of Rome, or just the opposite, it was Rome that dreamed of the silkworm.
10. The Tugai forest breeze: the harmony of silk and porcelain notes.
11. The Han Princess Liu Xijun: the Wusun Kingdom's Sappho married to a vast, limitless homesickness.
12. Standing below a statue of Kumarajva, it occurs to me that perhaps it was his masterful translation that saved Buddhism.
13. The three Mahasaattvas on their way to seek an audience with the emperor were on the opposite path as the Three Wise Men.
14. If Emperor Wu of the Han Dynasty had known Ferghana horses were sick horses, would the *History of Dawan* need to be rewritten?
15. The person making offerings in the mural has long, slender eyes.
16. Pagodas: the desert's navigation system.
17. What a pity! Gan Ying saw the sea, but he didn't know which sea it was.
18. Mandra petals: 5 *zhu* each.

19. 玄奘讲经处的颓垣，升起月牙的耳轮。
20. 在坎儿井的黑暗迷宫里，流水寻找着明媚的葡萄园。
21. 迁徙——从梵语、吐火罗语、回鹘语到汉语；逃过战火和千年的遗忘，《弥勒会见记》像凤凰飞入我的视野。
22. 又一首《醉汉木卡姆》：木塞莱斯酒啊，冰冷的美人，快浇灭我对你的欲火吧！
23. 在喀什，沈苇对我说：有白杨树的地方就会有人烟。

19. Over the crumbled walls where Xuanzang preached, the crescent moon's ear rises.
20. Flowing water seeks radiant vineyards in the dark labyrinth of Karez's wells.
21. Migration—from Sanskrit, Tocharian, and Uighur to Chinese, having escaped the furies of war and a thousand years of having been forgotten, *A Study of Maitreya* is a phoenix flying into my field of vision.
22. Another "Drunk Man's Muqam": Ah, Merceles wine, freezing beauty, hurry and drown the lust I feel for you!
23. In Kashgar, Shen Wei says to me: where there are white poplars, there will also be signs of human life.

克孜尔三章

1

石窟如蜂房。那穿石的人是谁？
火星四溅，像羲和敲打着太阳。

水，绕过山前，它在笑，
水中有一朵莲花在笑。

沙瑟瑟作响，唿哨来自胡杨林。
骆驼的脚，人的脚，
在起伏的沙上留下热吻。

我在断崖上搜寻，一个名叫
惠勒的龟兹人的题字，

那个内心朗照着佛光的匠人，
我似乎看见他的虬髯了。

2

灿烂如花，诸佛的脸，
在青金石粉和朱砂的斑驳虹彩中，
趺坐着降服了群魔。画工里
有一位来自叙利亚。

悉达多，怎样的一个人！
游历了恐惧和疾病的众多地狱，
善哉！当苦行结束，一只碗，
从陌生妇人的手中递过来。

Kirgiz: Three Chapters

1

The grottos are like a honeycomb. Who's that passing by the stone?
Mars shatters like Xihe drumming the sun.

Water circles in front of the mountain; it's laughing,
the lotus in the water is laughing.

The sands hiss, a whistling coming from the desert poplar forest.
Camels' feet, people's feet
leave hot kisses on the undulating sands.

I'm on the precipice searching for an inscription by
someone named Hui Le from Qiuci.

I seem to see his curly beard,
this artisan whose heart shone with Buddha's light.

2

Splendid like flowers, these various Buddha faces
in the mottled iridescence of lapis lazuli powder and cinnabar
sitting in lotus, surrendering to a group of demons.
One of the painters is from Syria.

Siddhartha, what a person!
He traversed the numerous hells of fear and illness.
How excellent—when his ascetic practice ended
a female stranger's hands passed him a bowl.

——颤栗！这从未有人尝过的甘甜，
像星辰、树木与众生的曼佗罗，
在盛满乳糜的碗中盛开，
他走了出去，那边就是鹿野苑。

3

千年一瞬——在佛的指尖。
经历着剥蚀，摧毁和外国人的偷盗，
凿痕像山的肋骨裸露着；

失去了雕像的空底座，
只能交给游人去践踏，
（且导游自称改宗者的后裔。）

更多依赖物质的人，空心人，
已陆续来到，仰起头，
被飞天的长袖舞得头晕目眩。

但后山的千泪泉——我听说，
在每一个虔敬的早晨，仍将洒下
兜率天的极乐梵音。

Tremble! This sweetness yet untasted by anyone,
like stars, trees, and a mandala of all living things
blooming in a bowlful of ghee porridge.
He walked out and the Sarnath deer park was there.

3
A thousand years in an instant in Buddha's fingertips
underwent corrosion, destruction, and theft by foreigners.
Chiseled scars are like the mountain's exposed ribs.

The empty bases of lost sculptures
are merely left for travelers to trample on,
(and the tour guide calls himself a convert's descendant).

Even more people reliant on matter, mindless people
arrive in succession, raising their heads,
dazzled by flying Apsara's dancing sleeves.

But I've heard that the thousand-year spring behind the mountain
still sprays down the Bliss Mantra of Tushita
every reverent morning.

神话，昆仑，雪

进山后下起了大雪。我们本是去看冰川的，登上高处的豁口，封存万古的奇景再度被封存起来，突然而至的雪修改了群山的容貌，使这个神秘的区域更加神秘莫测了，边界已不复存在。几只牦牛向塔松林那边蠕动，很快就变成了雪球；乌鸦似乎为了某种征兆而飞来，匍匐在耀眼的雪地上，谁能肯定它们不是乔装打扮的青鸟呢？

我知道我永远到不了昆仑山，因为作为"帝之下都"的那座山，只不过与面前的这一座有着相同的音节。虽然那儿也有河流，但环绕着的作为界河的弱水，连羽毛也不能浮起，像希腊的厉司河一样，只有死者的幽灵能泅渡过去，开天辟地以来，据说除非有后羿之德，任何人也休想越过这深渊，进入那众神聚居的光辉国度。

山上的悬圃足以让巴比伦的空中花园逊色，在芬芳四溢的金枝玉叶中，生长着不死之树。秦始皇梦想过，汉武帝梦想过，多少文人学士渴望借助秘密的修炼通达朝向它的路径，最终都无功而返。倘若你胆敢一试，吃人的窫窳不可能放过你，何况比司芬克斯怪物更可怕的、长着虎牙的西王母呢。然而，正是对丹药的迷狂，诞生了道教的西王母崇拜（不要忘记，"婉衿"这个温柔的名字也是属于她的。）在山下的小村庄奥伊塔克，药材铺里堆满了形形色色的动物骨骼和稀有植物的花叶，给人以一种幻觉，似乎某个不死药的配方一直在民间秘密流传着。

Myth, Kunlun, Snow

After we entered the back of the mountain a heavy snow began. We were originally going to see the glacier. When we'd climbed up to a clearing, the marvels that had been sequestered for eons were sequestered once again. Unexpected snow altered the appearance of the mountains and made this mysterious area even more unfathomable, the boundaries ceasing to exist. A few yaks inched toward the pine forest pagoda and quickly turned into snowballs. The crows flew over, seemingly as some sort of omen, and crept across the dazzling snow. Who could say for sure that they weren't the black messenger birds in disguise.

I knew I'd never get to Kunlun Mountain, because that "mountain under the emperor" merely shared the same pronunciation as the mountain in front of me. Even though there's also a river there, on the border, even a feather can't float. Just like Greece's Lethe, only the ghosts of the dead can swim across it. Since Pangu split open the sky, it's said that no one except those with the virtue of Hou Yi should even think of crossing this abyss to enter the radiant country where deities converge.

The hanging gardens on the mountain put the hanging gardens of Babylon to shame. In the permeating fragrance of gold branches and jade leaves, there is a tree that never dies. Emperor Qin Shihuang dreamed of it, and so did Emperor Wu of the Han dynasty. Countless literati longed to find the path with the help of secret Daoist practices, but in the end they all returned in failure. If you dared to make an attempt, there's no way the man-eating Yayu would let you pass, let alone the Queen Mother of the West, whose fangs are even more frightening than the sphinx. However, it was precisely the craze over cinnabar elixir that gave rise to the Daoists' worship of the Queen Mother of the West (don't forget, the gentle name Wan Jin, also belongs to her). In the village at the base of the mountain, Aoyitake, all sorts of animal skeletons and rare plants are piled high in the medicine shop. This gives one the illusion that an elixir recipe has been secretly passed down.

神话的印记毕竟深深烙在了这片曾经被称为鬼方的土地。我走向采玉人离去后留下的河谷，山峦向西逶迤。那个巨大的裂口或许就是愤怒的共工与颛顼大战时撞坏的，山崩地裂的余响仿佛还在不断传来；一些巨石酷似倒下的天柱的碎片，这里那里横躺着。大洪水也可能就是从这个裂口冲决而出……然后，腿有点瘸的大禹来了。

After all, traces of myths are deeply branded into this land that was once called Ghost Territory. I walk toward the valley left after the person searching for jade departed, the mountain ranges wing westward. Perhaps that giant chasm was broken apart when the God of Water waged war against Emperor Zhuan Xu. The landslide echoes still seem to come this way ceaselessly; some boulders strongly resemble the fragments of the pillars, lying here and there. The great flood might have also burst forth from here. . . . Then, Yu, with his partially lame legs, arrived.

迷楼

观音山上，老人指点一处禅院，称此
地曾是隋炀帝迷楼旧址，因有感。

镜中，俯仰的螺钿乱抖，
嬉笑又追逐，取悦着皇帝。
曲房密室洞开仿真的花烛夜。

如果献上金枝和玉兽的人，
只为一睹运河上缓缓驶来的御船，
又何必惊异于宫苑深处的流萤？

他老了，身体的拱桥涨满
欲望源源无尽的春水，
他抽空自己，在庞大帝国的羞处。

恨不能把天下都装进这门牖之中，
又恐怕大限已近，游廊太短，
且琼花那勾魂的美也可索命。

镜子吐出的弑者占据了四野。
他怕的其实是自己，从某个轮回中，
将脖子套向锦带，茫然竦惕。

Labyrinth Tower

On Guanyin Mountain, an old man pointed to a temple and said it was built on the
site of the labyrinth tower Emperor Yang had built during the Sui dynasty. Because
of this, I was moved to write this poem.

In the mirror, inlaid hairpins tremble, dipping and rising.
Playful laughter comes chasing again, trying to delight the emperor.
The secret chamber simulates a wedding night.

If the one who offers gold branches and jade creatures
does so just for one glance at the imperial boat slowly sailing in the canal,
why should he be surprised at the fireflies in the palace garden?

He's aging. The arched bridge of his body swells
with desire for infinite spring water;
he wears himself out in the shameful places of the vast empire.

He wishes he could cram the whole world into this door to enlightenment,
but he also fears the end of his life is drawing near. The corridor is too short,
and snowball viburnum's alluring beauty can be lethal.

The assassins the mirror spits out fill the surroundings, but
what he actually fears is that from some incarnation
he'll place the brocade cloth around his own neck, scared senseless.

钥匙笑吟吟

雪中出现的会是谁呢？
圣雅克塔上站着这座大城的瞭望者。
你笑吟吟转出街角，
拿着——像一个老水手，
两手空空时似乎也这么拿着
钥匙的允诺，它在雪中闪烁。

你家客厅的地板像甲板，
被某个善良的夜枭摇着，
在它的大氅下我赢得一夜的熟睡。
穿越了一些我体内的隧道和洞穴，
陡峭或平缓的心之纬度，
太阳爬上饰花铁窗栏。

你卧室里的灯还亮着，
书摊在枕边，肖像中的策兰
在你的夜中忧郁地望着你。
我又要走了，鞋带上的冰渣融化了，
我听见钥匙在锁孔里笑吟吟，
并照亮了远方的雪。

The Key Is Glowing with Joy

Who will appear in the snow?
As the watchman stands on the Saint-Jacques Tower,
you come smiling around the street corner
holding the key's consent like an old sailor—
Even when your hands are empty, you seem to be holding it.
The key glimmers in the snow.

The wood floor in your living room is like a boat deck
being rocked by a kind owl
beneath whose cloak I gained a night of sound sleep.
Steep and flat latitudes of the heart
passed through some of the tunnels and caves in my body,
and the sun climbed the ornamental railings.

The light in your bedroom is still on,
books are strewn around your pillow, and from his portrait,
Celan sullenly watches you in your night.
I'm leaving again. The bits of ice on my shoelaces have melted.
I hear the key giggle with joy in the keyhole—
it illuminates the distant snow.

秦始皇陵的勘探

七十万奴隶的劳作算得了什么？
在骊山苍翠的一侧，他们挖，他们挖。
再重的巨石终比不上强秦的课税，
撬不起的是公孙龙子的《坚白论》。

痴迷的考古学家在烈日下勘探，
且为我们复现出，无论过去、现在、
或将来，各种暴君的癖好：
生前的奢华，死后无限的排场。

七十万奴隶，七十万堆尘土。
上蔡的李斯还能到东门猎几回兔子呢？
阿房宫固然华美，经不住一把火烧，
肉体的永存有赖于神赐的丹药。

空旷的帝国需要一些东西来填满，
需要坚贞的女人为远征的夫婿而哭泣，
六国亡魂该听得见长城轰然倾颓吧？
该知道，地狱之塔奇怪的倒椎体。

但这深处的死亡宫殿却是有力的矩形！
在令人窒息且揣摩不透的中心，
我猜测，祖龙仍将端坐在屏风前，
等待大臣徐福从遥远的渤海归来。

Exploring Emperor Qin Shihuang's Tomb

What does the labor of 700,000 slaves matter?
On the green side of Li Mountain they dug and they dug.
In the end, the heaviest boulders couldn't compare with the Qin's
        mighty levies;
what can't be pried open is Gongsun Long's *Discourse on Hardness
        and Whiteness.*

Obsessed archaeologists explore under the scorching sun,
yet all that persists in the memory, whether past, present,
or future, are the various addictions of despots:
their lavishness while alive, their unbounded extravagance after they die.

700,000 slaves, 700,000 piles of dust.
How many more times can Li Si of Shangcai come and hunt rabbits
        at the East Gate?
The magnificence of the E'pang Palace can't bear even one burning.
The eternity of the flesh relies upon the cinnabar elixir the gods confer.

The empty empire needs some things to fill it up;
it needs chaste women to weep for their husbands on expedition.
Shouldn't deceased souls of the six countries hear the Great Wall's
        crumbling collapse?
They should know the strange inverted spine of hell's pagoda.

But the palace of death in this abyss is a powerful rectangle!
In its unfathomable suffocating center,
I'm guessing the Dragon Ancestor still sits upright before the imperial screen,
waiting for minister Xu Fu to return from the far off Bohai Sea.

而机关密布中的弩矢是否仍能射杀？
肱着身，模拟百川和大海的水银，
柔软且安详地熟睡着，一朝醒来，
会不会吐出千年的蛇信啮咬我们？

隔着木然的兵马俑，在相邻的坑道里，
殉葬的宫女和匠人吸进了最后一口空气。
封墓的瞬间，透过逆光，他几乎看见
一只侧身的燕子逃过了灭顶之灾。

But can crossbows still kill in dense institutional cover?
Simulating the mercury of the rivers and seas,
waking one morning after such soft and serene sleep,
will it stick out a thousand-year-old forked snake tongue and bite us?

In a tunnel adjacent to the stoic terracotta soldiers,
palace women and craftsmen buried with the dead took their last breaths.
The instant the tomb was sealed, in the backlight, he could almost see
the profile of a swallow who'd escaped being buried alive.

苍山

十九座奇峰护佑着一个国家，
十八条溪涧像泪腺逸出，
那万古不易的巍峨与葱茏。
林下青冢，杜鹃与兰花绚烂，
水淋淋的太阳升上洱海的妆台。
农夫在阡陌间直起身，
苍山就在他的脸上呵气。
马帮过桥时，年货进了村，
土地不死，多彩的衣裳酡酊。
又一个外乡人站在感通寺的山门外，
通报自己餐风饮露的姓名。
乌鸦绕塔三匝，大雪落下来，
引领我把头抬得更高一些。

Cangshan Mountains

Nineteen peaks protect a country,
eighteen streams overflow like tear ducts—
that immutable loftiness and verdure.
Green burial mounds beneath the forest, cuckoos and orchids bedazzle.
The drenched sun rises over Erhai's vanity table.
The farmer stands up straight between paths,
Cangshan exhales onto his face.
As the caravan of horses crosses the bridge, the New Year's merchandise
        enters the village.
The land doesn't die, colorful robes are intoxicated.
Yet another out-of-towner stands outside the Gantong Temple gate
announcing their name of hardships in travel.
Crows circle the pagodas three times. Heavy snow falls,
arousing me to lift my head higher.

庭园劳作

山色不改，林梢吐纳
如丝的薄云。你站在木梯子上，
惦记起弥渡这个地名。
几只陶罐安详的样子，
似梦见了的水和土，
或几尾山涧里自在的红鱼。

静养的日子，有一种东西
在天上张望。薄云聚散着，
新迁的候鸟似乎患上了晕陆症。
几天来我注意到，
通过你殷勤的手指，
那棵山茶树的嫩蕾
开始了热烈的燃烧。

高原X光透视我们，
苍山与洱海之间的缓坡地带，
像太阳神的一道赦令。
蝴蝶迷乱的过渡在须臾完成，
人却需要更多的劳顿，
且让江湖郎中的火罐，
永作了孤寂的抚慰。

黄昏星刺激起炊烟与犬吠。
山后，雪域的无人区，
一只鹰安稳地收起了翅膀。
我的阅读已近尾声。
从木梯子上下来的你，
与房东太太说着话，
洗净了最后一片山茶树叶。

Working in the Garden

The mountain scene doesn't change. The branch tips spit out and receive
thin threadlike clouds. You stand on the wood ladder
contemplating the place named Midu.
The serene appearance of a few clay pots
is like having dreamed of water and soil,
or a few free red fish in the mountain stream.

On relaxed days, there's something
looking around in the sky. Thin clouds gather and disperse.
The migratory birds seem to be suffering from landsickness.
For several days I've noticed
that because of your attentive fingers
the buds on the camellia tree
have begun burning ardently.

The highland's X-rays examine us.
The gently sloped area between Cangshan Mountains and Erhai Lake
is like a pardon from the sun god
The butterflies bewildering transition happens in a flash
but people have to get more worn out.
Let the cupping jar
forever act as the lonely consolation.

The evening star provokes kitchen smoke and dogs' barking.
On the back of the mountain, in the region without any people,
an eagle smoothly brings in its wings.
My reading is already nearing its end.
You, coming down from the wooden ladder,
are talking to the landlord's wife,
washing clean the last camellia leaves.

蓝桉

河带走了传说，
人不断地告别。
汁液回旋，星星熄灭。
山谷的早晨从井底升起，
树下的女人倘若不被香气
击毙，就神秘地怀孕。

花催开一季的丧葬，
正当谷物尚未被河神充盈，
离此不远，死者思忖过
羽化成一只猫头鹰后的生活；
摇篮的动静牵系入睡的手，
门轴梦见转动它的人，
月光激起了水波。

尸灰瓮的绿釉滴着春光，
沙取代香枕的柔软，
没人见过的叶子取代了刀刃。
采撷的手指细长，
本身是植物。
她在烤烟房的塔楼上眺望
不久将要迎娶她的村落。

Blue Eucalyptus

The river carries legends away
and people endlessly part
Sap moves in circles and stars are extinguished
The valley morning is raised from wells.
If the woman under the tree isn't killed by its fragrance
she'll mysteriously become pregnant.

Flowers make a season of burials bloom
at a time when grains haven't been nourished by the river god.
Not far from here, the dead reflect on life
after having reemerged as owls.
The cradle's movements drag the hand entering sleep,
the door hinge dreams of the person turning it,
and moonlight stirs up waves.

The green glaze on the urn of ashes drips spring radiance,
sand replaces a fragrant pillow's softness,
unseen leaves replace the knife blade.
The slender fingers picking leaves
are plants themselves.
She looks into the distance from the tobacco-churning tower
toward the village into which she'll soon be married.

弥渡的罐子

晚霞绽开礼花，
卖陶器的人出了西城门。
你把它们摆放在院子里，
安详，柔美，像睡着的黑天鹅。
"要是能带回这些滚圆的东西，
我们将给它们喂什么？"

在夜和死亡之沙来填满，
恨的石头来敲碎以前，
这些甄轮上飞旋出的手工之花，
透气如虹的釉——
从泰初的寂静里递过来，
一圈圈女娲的指纹清晰可辩，
将把星座的允诺
放在日子的托盘上。

它们将被带上飞机，大大咧咧。
来吧，来抱紧属于我们的土魂，
用心去喂它。

Midu Jars

Sunset clouds burst forth fireworks.
The pottery seller has exited the West City gate.
You arrange them in your yard,
serene and graceful like sleeping black swans.
If we bring back these round things,
what will we feed them?

Before the sands of night and death fill them
and the stones of hatred break them,
the handmade flowers whirling out from the pottery wheel
flow freely as rainbow glaze—
handed over from the quiet of the beginning of the world,
circle after circle of Nü Wa's fingerprints are distinct,
placing the constellations
onto the tray of days.

They'll casually be taken onto an airplane.
Come, come and hold tight the clay spirit who belongs to us.
Feed it with care.

中元节。双虹升上洱海

半个天空燃烧，
就为了这喷薄的好客之甜，
在目击者的眼睛里
织出两匹锦缎。
壮哉，金子的盟誓，
横贯高原湖泊的上空，
如独龙族妇人的脸，
烙着纹饰，
笑吟吟，出来迎迓。

我们站在缓坡上，
在蓝桉的香气里，
背对逝者的船型冢，
和吞云吐雾的苍山。

我们迈向那双重的拱门。

下面，烟草地开着小白花，
水在引水渠里汩汩地流。
濒临灭绝的弓鱼接受了一个
长着鸭蹼的夜叉的祝福，
入夜以前，
一只山羊将要被宰杀。

本主庙里，相貌堂堂的人物，
红脸的泥人，
弯弯的两道眉会说预言，
会为我们禳灾。

Ghost Festival: A Double Rainbow over Erhai Lake

Half the sky is burning,
just for this sweetness of overflowing hospitality,
it weaves two brocades
in the eyes of the onlookers.
How truly robust! A gold oath
traverses the sky over the highland lake,
like Derung women's faces,
branded with decorations,
smiling, coming out to welcome us.

We stand on the gentle slope,
in the blue eucalyptus fragrance
with our backs to the boat-shaped burial mounds of the deceased,
and the Cangshan Mountains swallowing clouds and spitting out fog.

We step toward the double arch.

Below, tobacco fields bloom with little white flowers,
water gurgles as it flows in the canals.
Bow fish on the verge of extinction accept
the blessings of a web-footed Yaksha.
Before night falls,
a goat will be slaughtered.

In the Benzhu Temple, there are characters with majestic appearances;
the red-faced clay people
with two curved brows can make predictions
and perform sacrifices for us to avoid calamities.

蟋蟀的口弦拨弄着
阴阳两界的复调，
弹出草丛。
你们，下凡的两姐妹，
迎面撞见手捧祭品的乡人
和初来乍到的卜居者。

你们也为逝者搭起了回家的桥。

The cricket mouth harp is playing
the polyphony of the two realms of yin and yang,
playing wild grasses.
You two sisters who've descended into the world of immortals
have accidentally run into the villager carrying offerings in his hands
and the newcomers looking for a place to live.

You've also erected a bridge for the departed to return home.

圆明园之冬

湖干涸
但仍有一个太阳在湖底燃烧
古树呻吟地下
冻土块迸起火星

施工者的铁锹下
帝国残片的釉色
依然青翠

数不胜数的
死去的蚌
像宫女们羞涩的冤魂
裸露了出来
而群鸦安详如太监
从远处朝这里观望着

你向湖心走去
你找着一只徒然的绣花鞋

Winter, Yuanmingyuan

The lake has dried up
but a sun still burns at the bottom of it
Ancient trees moan underground
Sparks burst forth from the cracks in frozen earth

Beneath construction workers' shovels
the glaze on the empire's pottery shards
is still green

Dead clams
Too numerous to count
lie exposed
like the shy ghosts of palace maids
And flocks of crows serene as eunuchs
watch from the distance.

You walk toward the heart of the lake
You're looking for a useless embroidered shoe.

父亲的迁徙

他们找不到你。在当年草草埋葬你的山冈，
风布好了迷魂阵，那片故土在漂移。
长得过于茂盛的蕨像梦中的植物，
拉扯下午的阴影。我们沿溪谷，缓缓走上来，
带着被抹去标志的记忆的黑地图，
紧随气喘吁吁的收尸人。

你躺在那些肥硕叶子的大氅下，
在死的庇护下你躲得很严实。
答应我们，父亲，出来吧。再也不用捉迷藏了。
你的纽扣像白垩纪的小海贝——
这家族的圣物也被小心安放在瓮中。
现在，我们让你再度迁徙，
飞行在迫害者的笑声够不着的地方。

My Father's Migration

They can't find you. On the small hill where they buried you in haste that year
wind has expanded the soul-trapping maze; that piece of the homeland is adrift.
The overly lush ferns are like plants from a dream
that drag along the afternoon's dark shadows. We walk slowly upward
along the valley, carrying the black map with erased markings,
following closely behind the panting corpse collector.

You lie beneath a cloak of corpulent leaves,
hiding safely under death's protection.
Answer me, Father, come out. You no longer need to play hide and seek.
Your buttons look like small Cretaceous shells—
the family's sacred objects have been placed carefully in the urn.
Now we're forcing you to move again,
to fly in a place the persecutor's laugh can't reach.

遗 忘

1

日晷。头颅。谁退藏于密？
谁的仪表画出虚妄的圆弧？
你眼睛的祭坛深陷着
在未来某个庞大建筑的对面

彗星落向木樨地时
倘若我是你，你或许就是他：一个尾数
她最后的回首穿过了
呦呦鹿鸣

2

雪的谐音喷涌
花，无痛地绽放
一朵催开了死亡的非花
是真的。它攀上了你的名字

痉挛的灌木下
道具般的脚趾涂着萤火虫的黑盐
也是这么被抬走了
像极了新近地震中的场面

Forgetting

1

Sundials. Skulls. Who retreats to hide in secret?
Whose appearance paints a fabricated arc?
The altar of your eyes is sunk deeply
across from some future giant building.

When the comet falls toward Muxidi,
if I'm you, then perhaps you're him: a remainder.
Her final glance back passed through
the deer's bleating.

2

Snow's homonym spurts.
Flowers painlessly blossom.
A non-flower that pushed death into bloom
is real. It climbs onto your name.

Spasms beneath the bush,
prop-like toes are smeared with the black salt of fireflies
and are carried away like this,
so much like the scene of an earthquake.

3

喷枪那闪电节奏的火舌
吻遍娇嫩的脸。清晨的水龙头
把夜的灰烬灌溉了又灌溉
结痂的将长成石笋，在心脏部位

一个失踪者走来，一个失踪太久的
失踪者，瘦长的手臂像唐·吉诃德
读秒的时间到了。你来读，像秒针一样读
履带的嘎嘎声里是什么已对峙了千年？

3

The airbrush, that lightning-tempo tongue of flame
kisses the lovely face all over. Morning's faucet
irrigates and re-irrigates night's ashes.
What has scabs will become a stalagmite in place of the heart.

A missing person comes over, someone who's been missing
for too long, his slender arms like Don Quixote's.
It's time to read the seconds. You read them, just like a second hand
        reads them.
What in the rumbling tank tread has already been standing in opposition
        for thousands of years?

西湖夜游

江南的三姊妹，宝石山的宝石
发如蝉翼脆薄，半遮着手臂的藕色
她们用风铎引导我，在五月里蒸发
焦急的友人逡巡山下，害着诗歌的恐高症
客问：月何时升起？左岸，尽那边
杭州嗡嗡的灯火汇入涌金的钱塘
我的游魂归来了吗？水哉，水哉
摇着香獐树，梳理城门的睫毛

从白堤到苏堤，人与湖相嬉戏
蚌的开合中，燕飞来，莺飞去
小径无人，一只猫像葛洪勤勉的弟子
独步西泠。太湖石远瞻湖心亭，雾的秘密
升起岛上。对岸，尽那边，气象球高悬
三姊妹下山来，在水上走
如鹤与风；而跨不过去的断桥请我留步
客问：她们可是你记忆的主人？

夜的磁波在黑暗的船桨上
碎成水银，艄公朗笑的须髯如雪
灯笼滑过水天之际，照见护栏里

West Lake Night Journey

Three sisters of Jiangnan, gems of Gem Hill.
Hair thin as cicada wings partially conceals their lotus-colored arms.
They use bells to guide me, and I evaporate into May.
An anxious friend paces at the bottom of the hill, suffering from
      poetry acrophobia.
The traveler asks: *When will the moon rise?* On the left shore, at the
      farthest point,
Hangzhou's humming lights enter the gushing metal Qiantang River.
Has my wandering soul returned? Water . . . water
sways the musk trees and combs the city gate's brows.

From the Bai Causeway to the Su Causeway, the lake and the people
      play and frolic.
In the opening and closing clam shells, swallows fly back and orioles
      fly forth.
The path is empty. A cat is like Ge Hong's diligent disciple
walking alone across Xiling. A Lake Tai stone gazes out
at the lake's central pavilion, and fog's secrets rise above the island.
On the opposite shore, at the farthest point, a weather balloon hangs
      in the air.
The three sisters come down from the hill. They walk on the water
like cranes and wind. And the untraversable Broken Bridge asks me to stay.
The traveler asks: *Are they masters of your memory?*

Night's magnetic waves shatter on dark oars, turning murky.
The whiskers in an old man's smile look like snow.
A lantern slips across the horizon, illuminating the shy new lotuses
      inside the rail.

娇羞的新荷。海誓山盟的、爱猜谜的三姊妹
像刚从雷峰塔出来的越剧人物
对前世与来生都浑然不觉。右岸，尽那边
一条船是空的，有外星人独钓月色
我醉了，抱着西湖这酒坛子

Pledging their eternal loyalty, these three riddle-loving sisters
are like characters in a Yue opera who've just emerged from
             Leifeng Pagoda
completely unaware of their past or future lives. On the right shore,
             at the farthest point,
a small boat sits empty. An extraterrestrial fishes alone for moonlight.
I'm tipsy. My arms clasp this wine jug, the West Lake.

口信

如果明天，黑色舰队从我的眼睛登陆
请在梦中为鸽子铺好床
并嘱咐它把眼睛转向东方

如果我化身犰狳，从侏罗纪赶来救火
请赞美用拨火棍款待它的人

如果我结结巴巴像石头
在寒冷的高地睡去
你要灵巧如流水，用一支歌把我淹没

如果地球的聋耳朵在闪电的神经末梢
听不见情人们悲伤的低语
请对他们说：要么守着银河示众
要么像海蛞蝓，自由地卷曲

如果绿衣人按响了门铃，你要祝福他
数到七，我就从彩虹里面出来

Oral Message

If tomorrow the black fleet lands from my eyes,
in a dream please prepare a bed for a dove
and remind it to turn its eyes to the east.

If I turn into an armadillo and come from the Jurassic fighting fires,
please praise the person who provided the fire poker.

If I stammer like a stone
and fall asleep in the frigid highlands,
you'll need to be as nimble as water, and submerge me in a song.

If the world's deaf ears on lightning's nerve endings
can't hear the sorrowful whispers of lovers,
please tell them: if we aren't exposed beside the Milky Way,
we'll roll up freely as sea slugs.

If the person in green rings the doorbell, bless him,
count to seven, and I'll come out from inside the rainbow.

用诗占卜

用一个被弃绝的词
从凶手那里夺回的词
颠倒卦象
双手握住最下面那个爻
让它动起来

将要来临的，我们知道你

广袤的夜，广袤的无名
你，异乡者，陨石形状的人
站在初地的边沿，如在十地
那里一座艮山
刺破大气层
一粒精子前来做客
进入橐籥

你召唤灯蛾，你召唤死者
你掘一口通向盐池的井
你敲打恐龙蛋，从中
取出一封来自玄武纪的信
读吧，读给我们听
我们知道
那结痂的祥瑞也是你的

用一个暗哑的词
盛放你的声音
把它拌入黏土，敷在伤口上
把星座的咒语也拌进去
眼睛的网所泄漏的
我们收在心的葫芦里

你，异乡者，为我们占卜！

Poem Divination

Use a cast off word,
a word seized from assassins
Reverse the hexagrams,
hands grabbing hold of the bottommost line
Make it move

You who are about to come, we know you

Vast night, vast namelessness
You, person from another place, meteorite-shaped person
standing on the edge of the first realm as if in the ten realms
A mountain there
pierces the atmosphere
A sperm that has come to visit
enters the furnace hollows

You summon the moths, you summon the dead
You dig a well that leads to a salt pond
You crack a dinosaur egg and pull out
a letter from Black Tortoise
Read it, read to us
We know
that scabby omen is yours as well

Use a silent word
to hold your voice
Mix it with clay, apply it to your wounds
Mix in the incantations of constellations
That which the net of the eye lets slip through
we will gather in the heart's gourd

You, person from another place, divine for us!

忆故人

我牵挂的客人披着雪斗篷，
说他来自某个久远，
从寒武纪，从伯吉斯页岩
和刺胞动物的嘴，
经历了最凄苦的流亡。
说他是我的同族，长着与我
相似的颅骨，浓浓的，纠在一起的眉毛。
他声音柔美胜似当初。
我请他坐下，谈谈，
他脱口说出醉人的话语：

　　　雪普降的天下盐
　我抽象地尝了尝。我的舌头纯化了
　人对世界的终极评价
　——甜。
　夸克，那只虚空的核桃，
　我剥开它，
　宇宙的心，就在黑云母的
　心中砰砰跳。
　鹤，我的姐妹，
　刚洗了澡，喷了点
　彩虹牌香水，
　正在夕照的那边等着。
　我宁愿赤足蹈雪，
　也不要伪装成真理
　混入永恒。

有福的人哪，勾魂家，
不可测度的亲人，
在元诗矿山上熬炼着

Missing an Old Friend

The guest I was concerned about wore a snow cloak
and said he'd come from some remote age,
from the Cambrian Period, from the Burgess Shale Formation
and the mouth of a Cnidarian
and that he'd been through the bleakest exile.
He said he was the same ethnicity as me
with a skull shaped like mine and thick, tangled eyebrows.
His voice was gentler than before.
I asked him to sit and talk
and he blurted out intoxicating words.

    I've abstractly tasted the salt
    the snow has let fall onto the earth. My tongue purified
    people's final judgment of the world—
    It's sweet.
    That quark, that hollow walnut,
    I peeled it,
    the universe's heart pounding
    in black mica's heart.
    My sisters, the cranes,
    had just finished bathing, applied
    a rainbow perfume,
    and were waiting in the sunset.
    I'd rather step barefoot in the snow
    than disguise myself as truth
    and sneak into eternity.

The blessed, the seducer,
the unfathomable relative
is on the mine of metapoetry smelting

云、药片和沥青铀里的女巫，
他走过的离乡路迤逦在长庚星的望远镜里。
我问他那边的清凉世界有什么不同，
雪花是否呼啸，如酩酊的蝴蝶？
他缄默不语，并起身告别，
四周顿时弥漫奇异的薄荷香。
而话语的余温如三叶虫的眼皮，
将埋入颅骨的脉状矿床下，
封存在乌有乡的失物招领处。
更多留给死亡破解的字谜，
漂浮着，被误解，被流传，
在大江南北。

clouds, pills, and the witch in bituminous uranium.
The road of exile he'd traveled wound through the evening star's telescope.
I asked him what was different about the clear and cool world there—
Did the snow whistle like drunken butterflies?
He kept silent and got up to leave.
A strange faint mint scent suddenly pervaded the air,
and the remaining warmth of our words was like a tribolite's eyelids—
to be buried beneath the vein-like deposits on the skull
and kept in the lost and found of nowhere.
More riddles for death to decipher—
floating, being misunderstood, and being retold
throughout the country.

雨后双廊的下午

——给叶永青和八旬的短信

拴在岸边的小船在摇晃中睡着了，
微波起伏，彷佛有人在水下摇橹。
除了欸乃这个词，没有别的词可以呼唤出
远山的暧昧和一座高山湖
泼溅到天边的绿。那里百万吨的云，
正朝这里涌来，彷佛
百万头母牛正被一个空行母
赶下山来，为了来庆祝
一座新屋的落成。这时，玉几岛上，
人人都换上新颜，人人都在忙碌；
七八个乡绅相互拱手，揖让，
谈笑酷似旧时代的鸿儒。
这时（也就是酉时），风车收起了呼哨的网罟，
芦苇的细茎平衡住飘落的草鹭。
一个婀娜在餐桌旁的美妇抬头一望，
云的仪仗队里，那空行母朝下一指，
百万道光芒便汇聚成瀑布，
彷佛喷香的醍醐，向着下界
那些个频频鞠躬的，葫芦状的头顶
缓缓地倾注。于是那水下的人
爬上船来，打了个寒噤，给自己倒了点酒。
整个双廊没人看见他
怎样偷走了这个酩酊而
遍地锦绣的下午。

An Afternoon in Shuanglang, after the Rain

—a text message to Ye Yongqing and Ba Xun

The small boat tethered to the shore falls asleep in the rocking.
The water ripples as if someone underwater is sculling.
Only the word splash can summon the green of the heavy clouds and mist
from the distant mountains and the green of the alpine lake that splashes
       onto the horizon.
A million-ton cloud surges from here to there, as if
a million cows are being rushed down the mountain by a dakini
to celebrate the completion of a new house. At this time on Yuji Island
everyone dons a new look; everyone is busy.
Seven or eight modern village scholar-officials grasp hands and greet
       each other,
talking and laughing like the scholar-officials from ages past.
At this time (early evening) the windmill has retracted its whistling nets.
The reeds slender stalks balance the herons, gently falling.
An elegant beauty beside the table raises her head and looks up.
In the procession of clouds, the dakini points one finger down,
and millions of light rays converge into a waterfall,
as if sweet ghee is heading toward the mortal world.
Those repeatedly bowing, gourd-shaped heads
slowly stream down. And so the person underwater
climbs onto the boat, shivers, and pours himself some liquor.
No one on Shuanglang sees
how he steals this heavy intoxication
and this beautiful afternoon everywhere.

寻隐者不遇

晨曦泄露了群山之间万古的静谧，
村庄如梯子架在狭窄的陡坡之上。
太阳照见烤烟楼和铁索桥，照见
蹲在屋脊中央憨态可掬的瓦猫。
我欣喜于山的一半在阴影中，
而生长着蓖麻、蝎子草和仙人掌的另一半
打开在回响着鹪鹩之翼的北窗外。
雨季来临时，向上窜的绿火
将撩拨他呆在山顶，看成群的彩虹倾泼而下。
小溪是不可或缺的，白天忙碌，
夜里将呢喃送到枕边，当他高卧。
峡谷的幽深诱人探秘，但现在是枯水期，
瀑布细如山魈的尿液，不再飘动。
我想象这块大石头是他曾经坐过的，
天外灾星作祟，他自与仙人从容对弈。
金丝猴倒挂在葛藤上方，
表演着漫不经心的高空杂技。
榛子滚落，彷佛始于上一纪的地裂。
锦鸡飞不远，总是弄出很大的声响，
当马帮从山下拾级而上。
第一个运送井盐出山的人已死了几个世纪，
有谁在意他是否投胎转世？
（他要是有乡愁，他就将在本乡还魂）

Visiting the Hermit but Not Encountering Him

The first glimmer of dawn reveals the timeless tranquility among
      the mountains.
The villages are like ladders hanging on the steep narrow slope.
The sun shines on the tobacco curing building, and the metal rope bridge,
and it shines on the charming tile cat in the center of the roof edge.
I'm happy that half of the mountain is shady with castor-oil plants, garden
stonecrops, and cactuses, and the other half opens to the north window
resonating with the baby firebird's wings.
When the rainy season draws near, the green fires scurrying upward will
provoke the hermit to stay on the mountaintop, and watch the rainbow
      clusters spill down.
The small creeks are indispensable, daytime is hectic.
At night, when he sleeps comfortably, they send murmurs beside his pillow.
The serene depths of the gorge entice people to explore the unknown,
      but now is the time when the water is low,
the waterfalls are thin as mandrill's pee, they no longer flow.
I imagine he sat on this large rock before.
Unearthly disasters haunt this place, but he's unhurriedly playing Go.
The golden snub-nosed monkey is hanging upside down on a tangle
of vines, performing careless acrobatics high in the air.
The hazelnuts tumble down, as if from a ground fissure in the last century.
The golden pheasants don't fly far, they always make a great deal of noise
when the caravan of horses walks up from the bottom of the mountain.
The first person to transport well-salt out of the mountains has been dead
      several centuries,
who cares if he's been reincarnated or not?
(If he's homesick, he'll return from the grave to this village)

在诺邓这边，家家户户的大铁锅
依旧冒着烟，将不可或缺的盐卤熬炼。

几杆瘦竹迎着风，两三只鹅
（山阴道士曾用来换字），唱着击壤歌，
正把胖身子挤进窄窄的池塘。
门虚掩着，松鼠告诉我主人不在。
一株制造闪电的楸树投下足够的阴凉，
瓜瓢搁在水槽边，斧头的柄
翘起在一堆木柴上方，坚硬，油亮，
没人知道它曾经飞翔在哪片林中。

Here in Nuodeng every household's wok is still
emitting steam, and boiling the indispensable brine.

A few slender bamboo stalks greet the wind, two or three geese
(whom a Shanyin Daoist once exchanged for calligraphy) are singing
the song of striking the earth, squeezing their fat bodies into
      the narrow pond.
The door is slightly ajar; the squirrels tell me the owner isn't home.
A lightning-producing tea plant casts sufficient shade.
The gourd ladle is next to the sink, the ax handle
is sticking up from the firewood, solid, shiny.
No one knows in which section of the forest it once flew.

Notes

Flowing Water
"Flowing Water" is the title of a *guqin* piece. It was included on a gold disc carried into space on the Voyager mission, along with various other musical compositions and human languages.

Emptiness
The translation of these lines by Odysseus Elytis is based on the Chinese version that Song Lin uses in the poem. The translation differs slightly from other English versions (see, for example, the translation by Edmund Keeley and Philip Sherrard).

Sunday Sparrows and **Chrysanthemums on the Sea**
Song Lin wrote both of these poems while he was in prison in 1989 for participating in the democracy protests.

Montparnasse Model and **The City Wall and the Setting Sun**
The *konghou* is an ancient stringed instrument.

To a Likely Alien
The Weaver Girl and the Ox-herder are two stars in the Milky Way. According to traditional stories, each year on the day of the Double Seven Festival, magpies build a bridge across the sky to reunite these two lovers.

Jiangyin Ditty
Xu Xiake (1587–1641) is a famous traveler and geographer of the Ming dynasty. Born in Jiangyin, his writings were collected in *Xu Xiake's Travelogue*.

Advice for a Young Poet

Bo Ya was a well-known *qin* player from the Spring and Autumn Period. The Daoist text *Liezi* includes a story about Bo Ya playing the *qin* and Zhong Ziqi being able to understand and appreciate everything Bo Ya expressed through his playing. When Zhong Ziqi died, Bo Ya broke his *qin* and vowed to never play again.

Liu Chen and Ruan Zhao are known as Daoist immortals from the Eastern Han dynasty. See Liu Yiqing's *Records of the Hidden and Visible Worlds*.

Song of Exploring the Waterways

Commentary on the Water Classic is a 40-volume masterpiece on the geography of ancient China. It was compiled by Li Daoyuan during the Northern Wei dynasty.

Yi is said to be the archer who shot down nine of the ten suns. See the *Classic of Mountains and Seas*, an ancient Chinese text and mythic geography that was likely written by a number of individuals between the 4th century BCE and the Han Dynasty (206 BCE–220 CE).

The black messenger bird is one of the mythical creatures mentioned in the *Classic of Mountains and Seas*.

The Islands of Immortals refer to Penglai, Fangzhang, and Yingzhou, three legendary islands in the Eastern Sea. See the *Records of the Grand Historian*.

Soul Mountain is the site where the "ten shamans rose and fell" in the *Classic of Mountains and Seas*.

Naked Country is referenced in the *Huainanzi*, a book on philosophy and statecraft dating from the Western Han.

Yu Gong is the name of a chapter in the *Book of History*.

The strategists refer to one of the Hundred Schools of Thought from the pre-Qin era.

The fisherman here refers to the hermit who appears in the Warring States poet Qu Yuan's work "The Fisherman."

Metal letters refers to a collection of writings attributed to the Southern Song painter and writer, Zheng Sixiao (1241–1318). A Song dynasty loyalist, Zheng is said to have compiled these into a work known as *History from the Heart*. Legend has it that he placed this collection into a water-tight metal box inside of a well. The box was discovered later in the Ming dynasty.

Song Yu was a poet from the state of Chu during the Warring States Period. The line, "Song Yu's dream interpretation skills satisfied the King of Chu" refers to King Qingxiang of Chu from the Warring States Period.

The mythic king of the waters is King Yu of the Xia dynasty.

Peach Blossom Spring refers to the Jin dynasty poet, Tao Yuanming's (Tao Qian) work of the same title—a utopian land where people existed in harmony with nature.

The erotic mountain ghost is a goddess from Qu Yuan's "Nine Songs."

The mysterious river chart refers to the patterns on mythical horses and dragons that Fuxi is said to have used to develop the eight trigrams in the *Book of Changes*.

Notes from Southern Xinjiang
Kumarajiva (344–413) was a Buddhist scholar and translator. He is regarded as being one of the most important translators of Buddhist texts from Sanskrit into Chinese.

The Ferghana horses' Chinese name means "blood-sweating horses." These horses were imported to China from Central Asia.

Gan Ying (Eastern Han dynasty, exact birth and death dates unknown). In the year 97, he was sent on a diplomatic mission to the Roman Empire but only got as far as the Persian Gulf.

Zhu are an ancient type of coin. In this poem, Song Lin is referring to those coins used in the Han dynasty that bear the seal "Five *zhu*."

Kirgiz: Three Chapters
Xihe is the goddess that gave birth to the ten suns.

Sarnath deer park is the site where Siddartha is said to have given his first Buddhist sermon.

Tushita is known as the highest realm among the heavens.

Myth, Kunlun, Snow
Yayu is a man-eating monster from Chinese mythology.

Queen Mother of the West is the goddess who lives on the mythical Kunlun Mountain.

Ghost Territory was the pre-Warring States period name for the region where the nomadic Xiongnu people lived.

Zhuan Xu is a mythological god from the same tribe as the Yellow Emperor.

Yu, or Yu the Great, is the mythological founder of the Xia dynasty and the individual responsible for taming the great floods.

Labyrinth Tower
According to history books, Emperor Yang of the Sui dynasty built the Grand Canal in order to view the snowball viburnum.

Exploring Emperor Qin Shihuang's Tomb
Gongsun Long was a member of the Pre-Qin Hundred Schools of Thought. His works were published in *Gongsun Long Zi*.

Li Si (280–208 BCE) was a statesman, writer, and calligrapher from the Qin dynasty.

Midu Jars
Nü Wa is the mythological goddess who repaired the pillars of heaven and created people from clay.

My Father's Migration
Written during the Grave Sweeping Festival, 2007.

Forgetting
The line "snow's homonym spurts" refers to blood, which is a homonym for snow in Chinese.

West Lake Night Journey
Ge Hong is a Daoist thinker from the Jin dynasty. His work in *The Master Who Embraces Simplicity* deals with alchemy and writing.

Visiting the Hermit but Not Encountering Him
The calligrapher Wang Xizhi was so fond of geese that a Shanyin Daoist once gave him a goose in exchange for his calligraphy.

The song of striking the earth is a song that supposedly passes down one of China's oldest poems. See *The Origin of Classical Chinese Poetry*, compiled by Shen Deqian in the Qing dynasty.

JINTIAN SERIES OF CONTEMPORARY LITERATURE

Flash Cards
Yu Jian
Translated by Wang Ping & Ron Padgett

The Changing Room
Zhai Yongming
Translated by Andrea Lingenfelter

Doubled Shadows
Ouyang Jianghe
Translated by Austin Woerner

A Phone Call from Dalian
Han Dong
Edited by Nicky Harman
Translated by Nicky Harman, Maghiel van Crevel,
Yu Yan Chen, Naikan Tao, Tony Prince & Michael Day

Wind Says
Bai Hua
Translated by Fiona Sze-Lorrain

I Can Almost See the Clouds of Dust
Yu Xiang
Translated by Fiona Sze-Lorrain

Canyon in the Body
Lan Lan
Translated by Fiona Sze-Lorrain

Something Crosses My Mind
Wang Xiaoni
Translated by Eleanor Goodman

October Dedications
Mang Ke
Translated and edited by Lucas Klein,
with Huang Yibing and Jonathan Stalling